THE ART OF LETTING GO

HOW TO LET GO OF THE PAST, LOOK FORWARD
TO THE FUTURE, AND FINALLY ENJOY THE
EMOTIONAL FREEDOM YOU DESERVE!

DAMON ZAHARIADES

ARTOFPRODUCTIVITY.COM

CONTENTS

PART III
**21 STRATEGIES FOR LETTING GO AND
MOVING ON WITH YOUR LIFE**

OTHER BOOKS BY DAMON ZAHARIADES

How to Make Better Decisions

14 proven tactics to overcome indecision, consistently make smart choices, and create a rewarding life in the process!

The Mental Toughness Handbook

The definitive, step-by-step guide to developing mental toughness! Exercises included!

To-Do List Formula

Finally! Discover how to create to-do lists that work!

The Art Of Saying NO

Are you fed up with people taking you for granted? Learn how to set boundaries, stand your ground, and inspire others' respect in the process!

The Procrastination Cure

Discover how to take quick action, make fast decisions, and finally overcome your inner procrastinator!

Fast Focus

Here's a proven system that'll help you to ignore distractions, develop laser-sharp focus, and skyrocket your productivity!

The 30-Day Productivity Plan

Need a daily action plan to boost your productivity? This 30-day guide is the solution to your time management woes!

The 30-Day Productivity Plan - VOLUME II

30 MORE bad habits that are sabotaging your time management - and how to overcome them one day at a time!

The Time Chunking Method

It's one of the most popular time management strategies used today. Triple your productivity with this easy 10-step system.

80/20 Your Life!

Achieve more, create more, and enjoy more success. How to get more done with less effort and change your life in the process!

Small Habits Revolution

Change your habits to transform your life. Use this simple, effective strategy for adopting any new habit you desire!

Morning Makeover

Imagine waking up excited, energized, and full of self-confidence. Here's how to create morning routines that lead to explosive success!

The Joy Of Imperfection

Finally beat perfectionism, silence your inner critic, and overcome your fear of failure!

The P.R.I.M.E.R. Goal Setting Method

An elegant 6-step system for achieving extraordinary results in every area of your life!

Digital Detox

Disconnect to reconnect. Discover how to unplug and enjoy a more mindful, meaningful, and rewarding life!

For a complete list, please visit

http://artofproductivity.com/my-books/

YOUR FREE GIFT

~

I'd like to give you a gift as my way of saying thanks for purchasing this book. It's my 40-page PDF action guide titled *Catapult Your Productivity! The Top 10 Habits You Must Develop to Get More Things Done.*

It's short enough to read quickly, but meaty enough to offer actionable advice that can make a real difference in your life.

You can get immediate access to *Catapult Your Productivity* by clicking the link below and joining my mailing list:

http://artofproductivity.com/free-gift/

In the following pages, we'll venture together down the long, sometimes bumpy, but ultimately rewarding road toward achieving emotional freedom. We'll gently examine the painful memories, resentments, disappointments, and regrets that burden you. To aid us in this process, I'll introduce you to a collection of tools that I've found to be helpful.

Onward.

NOTABLE QUOTABLES ABOUT LETTING GO

❧

66 Some of us think holding on makes us strong, but sometimes it is letting go.

— HERMANN HESSE

66 The truth is, unless you let go, unless you forgive yourself, unless you forgive the situation, unless you realize that the situation is over, you cannot move forward.

— STEVE MARABOLI

66 Life moves on and so should we.

— SPENCER JOHNSON

INTRODUCTION

~

Most of us are saddled with negative thoughts and emotions. Some of these stem from painful memories due to deeply-felt personal losses. Others arise from agonizing disappointments resulting from false expectations and shattered dreams. Still others flow from anger, resentment, and frustration caused by stresses and crises that batter us each day.

We carry these negative thoughts and emotions with us. As long as we do so, they impact our attitude, health, and relationships. They hamper us from doing our best work. They prevent us from making the best use of our time and attentional resources.

They serve as mental obstacles, perverting our perspective, impeding our productivity, and ultimately diminishing our quality of life.

Once we decouple ourself from the frustrations, regrets, and painful memories that burden us, we experience emotional freedom. It manifests in our behaviors, decisions, and level of self-awareness. It shows in our relationships with loved ones, friends, neighbors, and coworkers. It reveals itself in the quality of our work and the satisfaction we feel from having completed the work.

Once we let go of our bleak, defeatist headspace, it can no longer hold us back. Letting it go releases us to focus on the important things that truly matter to us.

But how exactly do we let things go?

Too often, "letting go" is presented as an overly-simplistic, worthless catchphrase that advocates living happily in the absence of stress. That's unhelpful. It's akin to telling a stressed-out person to "stop worrying."

In this book, we'll journey together through a step-by-step process designed to *train* you to let things go. You'll learn to adopt a mindset of non-attachment. The idea of non-attachment is often understood to mean abandoning material possessions. That's not our focus. Instead, we'll pursue non-attachment as it relates to the grievances, bitterness, and other psychological burdens that live rent-free in our minds. I'll share numerous strategies and techniques that have worked for me over the years. Each one will be accompanied by a simple exercise you can use to reinforce it.

Another important question: how do we identify negative thoughts and emotions?

We sometimes harbor and entertain them for so long

that they become a part of our identity. At that point, they become extremely difficult for us to recognize. We *believe* we've moved past our anger, regrets, and emotional pain, but instead they've burrowed so deeply into our state of mind that they're a repressed part of our mental landscape.

In the sections that follow, we'll resolve this issue, as well. You'll learn how to know when you're holding on to negative thoughts and emotions. You'll discover how to quickly identify them no matter how deeply they've burrowed into your mindset, attitude, and worldview. Once you've identified them, you can use the techniques we'll cover to get rid of them.

The Art of Letting GO is not a contemplative discussion. Rather, it's an actionable blueprint for overcoming the mental and emotional obstacles that are currently holding you back. We'll focus on techniques and strategies that produce quick, reliable results.

It's my sincere hope that this book will give you the tools you need to finally let go and experience the mental, emotional, physical, and even spiritual freedom that comes from adopting a mindset of non-attachment.

Damon Zahariades
Art of Productivity
March 2022

WHAT YOU'LL LEARN IN THE ART OF LETTING GO

~

The *Art of Letting GO* is a self-contained course. Part tutorial and part personal workshop, it will take you step by step through the entire process of becoming emotionally free by adopting a non-attachment mentality.

Many books address this topic by doing a deep dive into psychology. That's a good approach, and I'm certain it's beneficial for a particular type of reader. This book takes a different approach. We cover the material from a practical perspective, ensuring that it's easily accessible and immediately actionable.

Because there's a lot to cover, it's helpful to have a bird's-eye view of the material. To that end, here's a quick breakdown of what you'll find in *The Art of Letting GO*:

Part I

Before we can make serious progress toward letting go of the negative emotions, painful memories, frustrations, and regrets that burden us, we need to lay a foundation. In *Part I: The Upside of Letting Go*, we'll build that foundation.

We'll discuss what it actually means to let go of things. We'll also investigate the signs that suggest we're holding on to something that is harming our emotional health. We'll take a closer look at the advantages of abandoning our regrets, anger, and pain, and replacing them with self-compassion and empathy. We'll also examine the most common things people tend to hold on to despite the attendant emotional cost.

Finally, we'll explore how our minds resist letting things go.

Part II

Letting go isn't easy. If it were, there would be no need for this book. Unfortunately, most of us struggle with years of conditioning that "train" us to hold on to things.

In *Part II: The Most Common Reasons We Struggle to Let Go*, we'll scrutinize the most significant elements of this conditioning. We'll lay them bare so we can fully appreciate why it's so difficult to let things go, from the past and the present.

Understanding *why* we struggle to let things go is a necessary step toward reconditioning our minds. It's a crucial component to the process of slowly embracing an attitude of non-attachment.

what does this mean?

Part III

This is where you'll learn the techniques for letting go of the negative thoughts, emotions, disappointments, anger, and self-recrimination that are currently holding you back. *In Part III: 21 Strategies for Letting Go and Moving on with Your Life*, we'll cover dozens of tools you can put to immediate use.

This part of the book is filled with practical, use-it-now tools, tips, and advice. Each section is short, simple, and actionable.

It's natural to want to speed through this material. After all, it's highly applicable and promises quick results. However, I encourage you to adopt a measured pace, one that gives you plenty of time to fully learn each technique before moving to the next one. In my experience, that's the most effective path toward countering a preconditioned mindset and replacing it with a new, healthier one.

The Road Forward

As you can see, we have a lot to cover. But don't worry. Each section of *The Art of Letting GO* is tightly written. Each moves quickly, delivering its core advice in as little time as possible.

Allow me to make one suggestion: please take the time

to perform the exercises you'll find in *Part III*. Each is designed to reinforce the concepts introduced and discussed in its section.

The exercises won't take long to perform. All of them are simple and most can be completed in 20 minutes or less. Most importantly, performing them gives you an opportunity to apply the techniques rather than merely reading about them. In the end, they'll help you to enjoy maximum value from *The Art of Letting GO*.

If you're ready to commit to pursuing true mental and emotional freedom by letting go of regrets, resentments, grudges, and guilt, let's roll up our sleeves and take the next step.

PART I

THE UPSIDE OF LETTING GO

~

Regret is an inescapable part of life. We make mistakes. We make poor decisions. We experience consequential, meaningful losses, many of which we believe to have been avoidable.

But regret isn't without value. It serves a purpose. It teaches us lessons, helping us to avoid repeating the same mistakes and poor decisions. If we allow regret to fester, however, reliving our past blunders and choices over and over, it becomes an emotional obstacle. We end up creating a false narrative in our heads. This narrative tries to convince us that we're incapable of making *good* decisions and therefore undeserving of the things we desire.

At this point, we feel stuck. Disappointed. Frustrated.

Stressed. And worst of all, we feel this predicament is entirely our fault and that we lack the ability to make positive changes. We feel impotent.

The upside of letting go is that we can shed these feelings, reclaim our agency, and finally pursue our interests and desires free of needless emotional guilt and self-reproach. We can move forward with the expectation that good things can happen for us, and importantly that outcomes are largely in our control.

Of course, shedding our frustrations, disappointments, anxieties, and feelings of self-recrimination is easier said than done. They're usually deeply rooted in these five areas of life:

1. our relationships (with family members, friends, and spouses)
2. our health (physical and mental)
3. our personal development (educational, emotional, and spiritual)
4. our careers or business ventures
5. financial concerns

In the next few chapters, we'll build the foundation of adopting a non-attachment ethos. This new mindset will positively affect each of the above areas. You'll learn how to know for certain when you need to let something go, why you should immediately do so, and experience the rewards that are yours for the taking.

WHAT LETTING GO MEANS (AND WHAT IT DOESN'T MEAN)

66 There's an important difference between giving up and letting go."

— JESSICA HATCHIGAN

~

We hold on to things because they're important to us. When circumstances involving them change, we have difficulty making adjustments. Emotionally, we're unable to accept the new state of affairs.

For example, suppose your actions in the workplace cause you to lose your job. If being employed is part of your identity, it may be difficult to accept being fired. It's understandable to feel anger, disappointment, and even self-reproach if you regret your actions.

Or imagine that you and your spouse decide to divorce. If your marriage is important to you, its dissolution may be hard to come to grips with. Again, anger, disappointment, and regret are likely to bubble to the surface. As long as they remain there, you'll struggle to adjust.

Ideally, we would be able to confront these negative emotions, manage them in a healthy manner, and eventually move on with our life. For example, we'd get a new job. Or we'd meet someone new who becomes significant to us.

Too often, however, we cling emotionally to our past circumstances. We refuse to move on because we feel we can effect change that allows us to reclaim them. This is the bargaining stage of grief. It's natural, but also detrimental to our ability to move forward. It gives us a fallacious sense of control.

Letting go begins with accepting our new circumstances. Rather than clinging to a past we desperately want to reclaim, we embrace reality. We commit to no longer dwell on the past. We detach ourself from circumstances over which we have minimal influence.

For example, we accept that we've lost our job due to our own actions. We come to grips with the fact that our marriage has ended. And importantly, we recognize our inability to change these events. We transition from the bargaining stage of grief, where these events seem wrong to us, to the acceptance stage, where the pain of regret and disappointment can finally dissipate.

What Letting Go Doesn't Mean

Letting go is sometimes misunderstood as the avoidance of emotional discomfort. Rather than dealing with negative thoughts and emotions, they're jettisoned. This is a dangerous, unhealthy mindset to adopt because it leads to a perpetual state of apathy. By avoiding emotional discomfort, we end up embracing an attitude of indifference and even callousness.

We do so to protect ourself from stress, sadness, and emotional pain. Unfortunately, this frame of mind does more harm than good. We end up abandoning the opportunity to acknowledge these legitimate feelings and deal with them in a healthy manner.

The proper way to let go involves recognizing our negative thoughts and emotions, determining why we're experiencing them, and moving from the denial and bargaining stages to the acceptance stage of grief. Two important things happen during this process.

First, we develop emotional resilience. We learn to *manage* our emotions rather than suppress and avoid them.

Second, we adopt a mindset of non-attachment to the past. We acknowledge our feelings, investigate them, and ultimately give ourself permission to let them go, accepting our new circumstances. We recognize that attachment to the past is unhealthy, and *resolve* our emotional discomfort rather than simply pushing it away.

If we truly wish to let go of painful memories, regrets,

frustrations, and general unhappiness, we must confront these feelings head on. I'll share with you techniques that work in *Part III*.

HOW TO KNOW WHEN IT'S TIME TO LET GO

> Some people believe holding on and hanging in there are signs of great strength. (However, there are times when it takes much more strength to know when to let go and then do it.)

— ANN LANDERS

Our mind has the ability to conceal our emotional state. This ability is simultaneously a strength and weakness. In the beginning, it serves as a form of protection. If we're unaware of our emotional state, we can avoid feelings of angst and frustration as well as threats to our self-image.

Unfortunately, this avoidance quickly aggravates our emotional state. We remain unaware of how we feel, and thus fail to confront the negative thoughts that cause us stress and misery. If we fail to confront them, we are unable to properly manage them.

For this reason, it's important that we're able to recognize when negative emotions, and the circumstances from which they stem, are holding us back. Only then can we deal with them in a healthy manner and finally let them go.

With this in mind, here are several signs that suggest you're holding on to something that is negatively affecting your state of mind. If you experience any of them, it's important to investigate the reason. Ask yourself *"what am I holding on to that is causing me to feel this way?"*

You feel perpetually frustrated

The frustration may not be overt. It might be an undercurrent that bubbles just beneath the surface of your public guise throughout your day.

This feeling usually stems from a sense of helplessness. You feel unable to change the circumstances that trouble you. It can give rise to a host of other upsetting feelings, such as guilt, anxiety, and sadness.

You spend significant time agonizing about a particular incident

It's one thing to think about the past, recalling significant memories (recent or long passed). It's another thing entirely to dwell on a single memory that causes us emotional pain and unhappiness. Examples can include losing your job, getting divorced, or making a regrettable decision.

Our past contributes to our identity. It gives us a broader scope through which to view our current circumstances. It can also serve as a tool that helps us to solve problems and manage our emotions.

But sometimes we fixate on an unpleasant incident. It becomes distressing to us, which ironically causes us to become even more preoccupied by it. This single memory eventually dominates our attention.

You find yourself wallowing in self-pity

Self-pity can stem from a variety of internal and external factors. Examples include a relationship that has deteriorated, unfair treatment from our boss, an incident that causes us to feel victimized, or a goal that constantly seems out of our reach.

As with feelings of frustration, self-pity arises when we believe we're unable to control or influence a particular situation. We feel sorry for ourself because we feel we lack agency.

You continue to rationalize a decision or action despite evidence showing it was unwise

One of the ways we hold on to things that cause negative emotions to fester is to justify our decisions and actions, even when they prove to be reckless or imprudent.

For example, we might defend our decision to stay with a spouse who cheated on us despite the "salvaged" relationship making us feel miserable. We may rationalize assaulting someone who insulted us despite the fact that we now feel ashamed and embarrassed.

The effort to justify our decisions and actions springs from our ego. And that's a clear sign that we should evaluate our emotions surrounding the situation in question.

You feel emotionally drained

This feeling is a difficult one to recognize and assess. Emotional exhaustion occurs slowly. And because of its gradual escalation, it often goes unnoticed and therefore unmanaged.

It's akin to the proverbial frog that is placed in a pot of tepid water. If the temperature of the water is slowly increased to the boiling point, the frog will fail to perceive the danger. It will remain in the pot until it expires.

Emotional exhaustion is often misattributed to the daily stressors of our personal or work life — for example, our commute to the office or caring for a child who is throwing a tantrum. In reality, it often stems from stress, anxiety, and regret over a past circumstance that we're holding on to.

You can't remember the last time you felt happy

Chronic unhappiness doesn't stem from life's daily stressors. And while unhappiness *can* arise from being glued to social media, constantly acquiring material goods, and lack of socialization, these too rarely lead to *chronic* unhappiness.

If you cannot recall the last time you were happy, you may be clinging to a painful memory, deeply-felt loss, or regrettable and consequential decision made with false expectations. Your attention might be consumed by it to the point that it has obfuscated the small joys normally experienced during the course of a given day.

This feeling, if allowed to continue unaddressed, can open the door to depression and lead to emotional and social isolation.

What To Do When You Notice The Signs

It's important to examine why you're experiencing the negative emotions and feelings described above. The more quickly you do so, the better. If you allow them to remain unexamined, they'll continue to expand, preventing you from enjoying the emotional freedom that comes with letting things go.

In *Part III*, we'll explore numerous techniques that will help you to experience this freedom. But we have a bit more ground to cover in the next few sections to build a reliable foundation on which these techniques will stand.

10 REASONS WE SHOULD LEARN TO LET GO

" When we give ourselves the chance to let go of all our tension, the body's natural capacity to heal itself can begin to work.

— THICH NHAT HANH

We've touched upon the emotional freedom you'll experience when you let things go and adopt a non-attachment mindset. But let's dig more deeply. Let's take stock of the complete range of benefits you'll enjoy so you'll have a full appreciation for what's truly at stake.

#1 - Personal Growth

When we fixate on something, we devote our attentional resources to it. These resources are monopolized by whatever has caused us pain, anger, or disappointment in the past (or present).

When we let go of a painful or unpleasant memory, we free up these resources. This allows us to put them to use in pursuit of becoming a better version of ourself in every way.

#2 - Improved Mental Health

Clinging to painful memories puts significant strain on our confidence, self-esteem, and mental resilience. It slowly wears us down and can even set the stage for depression.

When we let them go, we remove this mental pressure. As a result, our confidence grows, our self-esteem strengthens, and we begin to rebuild our resilience against life's stressors.

#3 - Improved Physical Health

Remaining emotionally attached to past regrets, judgments, and even personal grudges puts significant strain on our bodies, as well. It raises our stress levels, increases our blood pressure, and can even impair our ability to sleep soundly.

When we detach ourself from the past, we alleviate this

physical pressure. Doing so allows our bodies to remain healthy, free of the unnecessary stress that burdened it.

#4 - Better Relationships

It's difficult to enjoy healthy relationships when we obsess over painful memories. The obsession hampers our ability to appreciate ourself. Moreover, it prevents us from truly appreciating others. As noted above, our attentional resources are monopolized by whatever has caused us pain.

Letting go frees us to focus on caring for ourself and others. We become more emotionally present, which helps us to become a better friend, spouse, and even coworker.

#5 - Less Focus On Pleasing Others

Our mental anguish often involves our decisions and actions that have displeased other people. These decisions and actions may have caused personal grudges, anger, and feelings of resentment.

When we let go of the past, we give ourself permission to no longer focus on pleasing others. Instead, we can focus on making decisions that prioritize our own needs and make the best use of the resources at our disposal.

#6 - Greater Courage

The more we fixate on our regrettable decisions and actions, the more fearful we become about repeating them.

This fear can build to the point that we become unable to make even small decisions or take small steps forward.

When we stop obsessing over our past mistakes, we can begin to reasonably evaluate their consequences. In most cases, these consequences are far less significant than we had imagined. Recognizing this fact emboldens us to take action in the future.

#7 - Improved Adaptability

When we cling to a painful past, we become mentally stuck in that past. Unrealized goals, failed relationships, and previous losses and frustrations dominate our headspace. This makes it difficult for us to accept and adapt to changes in the present.

When we let go, we become more receptive to change. We become more adaptable. This benefits us as changes in our circumstances are often the precursor to personal growth and happiness.

#8 - Greater Appreciation For Daily Joys

Fixating on the past prevents us from enjoying the present. The small, joyful experiences that happen during the course of each day escape our notice. We miss opportunities to share a laugh with friends, to enjoy a short walk outdoors, and to lose ourself for a short time in a captivating novel.

Letting go frees us to appreciate these tiny pleasures.

Because we're no longer fixated on painful memories and frustrations, we can savor the small delights and little rewarding moments of happiness we once neglected.

#9 - More Empathy for Others

When we're preoccupied by our own pain, loss, and regret, we're unable to fully empathize with others' pain, loss, and regret. The more we obsess over our own pain, the less we can understand and sympathize with the pain of our friends, loved ones, and coworkers.

When we commit to letting go, we free ourself to relate to others' emotions. We become more able to appreciate their perspectives and understand their feelings. This helps us to feel more connected to those around us. We become better able to celebrate their triumphs and offer encouragement when they feel defeated.

#10 - Emotional Independence

Clinging to a painful past prevents us from finding joy in ourself. We begin to look externally for even a modicum of happiness. We can even become dependent on others to fuel our interests, reinforce our self-esteem, and provide mental stimulation.

When we let go of the past, we give ourself the freedom to recognize ourself as being in control of our personal happiness. We accept that we don't need to rely on others to feel positive about ourself and our circumstances.

The Hard Work of Letting Go

As you can see, there's a lot at stake. It's not an exaggeration to say our present and future happiness depends on our commitment to let go of the regrets, disappointments, grievances, and anger that are holding us back.

Letting go isn't easy. As I mentioned, if it were, there would be no need for this book. But doing so *is* possible, regardless of your circumstances or your past.

While everyone has a unique past with distinctive emotional pains and anxieties, we share many common stressors. At least on a surface level, we hold on to many of the same things. In the following section, we'll quickly examine the most common things people obsess over that ultimately hold them back. Fair warning: you may recognize a few in your own daily struggles.

TOP 20 THINGS WE SHOULD LET GO

" To let go is to release the images and emotions, the grudges and fears, the clingings and disappointments of the past that bind our spirit.

— JACK KORNFIELD

Holding on to painful memories isolates us from others. Even when our friends and loved ones recognize our pain and try to help, our emotional suffering seems like it must remain a solitary affair. That leads to loneliness and despair. Left unresolved, the isolation we experience grows to the point that we feel no one can relate to our pain.

In reality, people agonize over many of the same aspects of life. We hold on to painful memories surrounding similar circumstances. We cling to negative emotions involving similar regrets, losses, and disappointments. There's solace in recognizing that others have experienced — and are currently experiencing — distressing feelings and situations that are similar to our own.

With that in mind, here are the top 20 things people anguish over. These are the issues that monopolize their thoughts, batter their optimism, and rob them of joy. These are the things that routinely prevent people from enjoying true happiness and emotional freedom.

What follows isn't an exhaustive list. Not even close. But it *does* comprise many of the universal sources of emotional suffering over which we have limited control. Don't be surprised if you find yourself nodding and thinking *"Oh, that's definitely me."*

#1 - Failed relationships

Failed relationships are difficult to get over, even if we try to convince ourself otherwise. We naturally mull over them and scrutinize the reasons they broke down. We often blame ourself, even if we did everything possible to save them.

It's natural to feel attached to broken relationships, at least for awhile. But eventually, we must find a way to let them go in order to move on with our life.

#2 - Toxic relationships

Toxic relationships seem like they should be easy to let go. After all, they cause us stress and anxiety, and there's a marked absence of respect and trust. Yet these relationships are often the most difficult to walk away from. The partners become emotionally dependent on one another, encouraging each other to stay despite their mutual misery.

It's impossible to experience emotional freedom while mired in toxic relationships. The longer we tolerate them, the longer we rob ourself of the opportunity to find healthier relationships and the happiness that accompanies them.

#3 - Jealousy

Jealousy springs from feelings of insecurity and envy. We feel insecure about the possibility of losing something we currently enjoy in our life. Or we envy others' good fortune.

Most people think of jealousy in the context of relationships, but it can also involve our careers, possessions, and others' circumstances. Left untamed, it often develops into feelings of resentment, inadequacy, and even shame, all of which harm our self-esteem.

#4 - Past failures

We tend to internalize our failures. Failed relationships, business ventures, investments, competitions, tests, and interviews stay with us. We agonize over things we could have done differently to produce better results.

Reviewing our failures is healthy. It allows us to avoid repeating mistakes. But when we obsess over them and are unable to make peace with them, we invite feelings of self-condemnation. This usually leads to guilt and shame, and eventually we question our efficacy.

#5 - Past regrets

Feelings of regret stem from choices we believe we made poorly. For example, we married the wrong person, purchased a house in a bad location, or picked the wrong major in college. We hold on to these regrets because we believe that our life would be markedly better if only we had made different decisions.

But the past cannot be changed. Regrets over past choices become emotional baggage and eventually a part of our identity. They cause us to doubt our competency, negatively impacting our self-esteem.

#6 - Past misfortunes

All of us experience misfortune. We lose our job, suffer a debilitating health condition, or become involved in a serious traffic accident. We get mugged, our vehicle is vandalized, or our home is burgled. When such events occur, it's natural to feel sorry for ourself. We may even wonder *"Why do these things always happen to me?"*

While this can be cathartic, it can also open the door to feelings of hopelessness. Unless we decide to let go of our misfortunes, we begin to perceive ourself as a victim of bad luck. Once we identify as a victim, we lose our sense of personal agency.

#7 - Unachieved goals

It's easy to get emotionally attached to our goals and aspirations. We begin to visualize achieving them. We imagine the sense of accomplishment and satisfaction we'll experience as a result. But this attachment is a double-edged sword. When we fail to realize our goals, we feel frustrated, disappointed, and ineffectual.

Failed goals can serve as powerful lessons. We learn about our strengths and shortcomings. We find out whether our goals were realistic. We learn how to improve our focus and execution. But we risk missing these lessons entirely if we're unable to emotionally detach from our failed outcomes.

#8 - Judgments of others

None of us enjoys being judged by others. We dread the possibility that our friends, loved ones, coworkers, and even strangers might consider us to be lazy, stupid, crazy, or useless. This dread, if we allow it to persist, can eventually cause us to fear and avoid making substantive decisions or taking significant action. We attempt to protect ourself by refusing to decide or act.

When we fixate on others' perceptions of us, we implicitly allow them to make our decisions for us. Our life is no longer our own. And our emotional health becomes dependent on what others think of us.

#9 - Others' grudges and disdain

We naturally want other people to respect us. But we're almost certain to cause some to feel bitterness and resentment toward us. Such feelings develop when people believe they've been wronged by us in some way, even if our doing so was unintentional.

Because we feel a sense of unease when someone is upset with us, grudges trouble us. We want to rectify things. This is, of course, a noble and worthwhile endeavor. But we can only exert limited influence. We can explain ourself. We can apologize. We can ask for forgiveness. But if someone's grudge cannot be remedied, we must let it go to protect our mental and emotional health.

#10 - Control over everything

We want to be in the driver's seat. We like to believe that we're the author of our circumstances. Exerting control gives us confidence that outcomes are a result of our influence.

The problem is, external events usually lie *outside* our influence. Control over them is largely an illusion. The biggest problem is, maintaining this illusion is mentally exhausting. When we surrender our desire to control everything around us, we become more inclined to accept unfavorable circumstances. We also develop the ability to adapt and respond to such circumstances in an emotionally healthy manner.

#11 - The expectation to be happy all the time

Most of us want to be happy. Happy with our spouses. Happy with our careers. Happy with our current state in life. But it's important to recognize that we can't be happy all the time. Continual happiness is a mirage because suffering is a part of life. We suffer stress, misfortune, hardship, and often both emotional and physical pain.

When we let go of the expectation to feel happy all the time, two important things happen. First, we become more willing to acknowledge our unhappiness. This is an important step toward figuring out — and either resolving or accepting — the things that bother us.

Second, we become less inclined to negatively compare ourself to others. As we start to appreciate the authenticity of our own emotional state, we begin to realize that everyone experiences unhappiness. We accept that others' appearance of happiness is often just a facade. Rather than envying them, we become better able to empathize and connect with them.

#12 - Anger

We feel angry when we're mistreated, threatened, ridiculed, invalidated, or shown contempt. While our anger may be justified, it's exhausting to hold on to. It takes a lot of energy to remain angry.

So why do we do it? Staying angry means we don't have to admit we're feeling emotionally wounded. It also gives us a sense of control as only we can decide when to stop being angry. And sometimes, the anger becomes part of our identity. We begin to use it as a tool to influence others.

When we let go of anger, we experience healthier relationships, less stress, and better mental and physical health. And we become better able to express our feelings to others in a constructive manner.

#13 - Shame

Shame stems from our perceived failure to measure up to an ideal image of ourself. For example, we behave in a way that we know to be inappropriate and feel embarrassed as a result. Or we make a terrible decision, one that we knew from the outset to be terrible, and feel regretful. Or we do something that we know is reprehensible and consequently experience remorse.

We hold on to shame when we avoid dealing with it. We avoid confronting the reasons we feel ashamed, and therefore never take the time to forgive ourself.

Letting go of our shame allows us to accept that we're imperfect and make mistakes. It also helps us to be more present in our current circumstances rather than trapped emotionally in the past. And it gives us an opportunity to challenge our assumptions regarding what constitutes a legitimate reason to feel shame in the first place.

#14 - Others' opinions

Many opinions are beneficial to us. Some provide useful and constructive feedback. Others offer insight we would otherwise overlook. These points of view can improve our performance, boost our creativity, and help us to recognize personal deficits and situational roadblocks.

But it's possible to become so reliant on others' opinions that we become unable to act on our own. Immobilized by fear, we seek validation from others for every decision and action.

When we let go of others' opinions, we begin to experience greater confidence in our own efficacy. We also enjoy the satisfaction and happiness that accompanies self-validation.

#15 - Unflattering comparisons to other people

It's natural to compare ourself to other people. Such comparisons provide helpful feedback regarding what we want to achieve. We recognize others' success in an area of life that interests us and can model their decisions and actions to achieve similar results.

The problem lies in comparing ourself in ways that make us feel jealous and resentful. If we feel we lack the power to achieve the same success we see in others, we end up feeling inadequate and depressed. For example, imagine that someone on Instagram constantly posts pictures of themselves in exotic locales while we're stuck at home. This makes us feel envious and inferior.

Letting go of these unflattering comparisons frees us from the emotional pain that stems from feeling ineffectual. When we stop caring that other people live better lives (often an illusion in and of itself), we start to appreciate the aspects of our own life that truly matter to us.

#16 - Perfectionism

The obsession to be perfect can stem from a variety of sources. For example, some of us fixate on it as a way to maintain control in the face of uncertainty. Others pursue it as a means to avoid criticism, blame, and judgment from other people. And still others try to be perfect in response to their own internal feelings of inadequacy.

Whatever its origin, perfectionism always leads to our

dissatisfaction. If we believe that being perfect is the only way we'll be happy, we guarantee our perpetual unhappiness.

When we stop trying to be perfect, we experience less anxiety, enjoy more creativity, and become more inclined to take purposeful, calculated risks. And importantly, we free ourself from the emotional burden of constantly striving for others' approval.

#17 - Circumstances you can't change

Once something happens to us, it becomes a part of our past. We cannot change the fact that it happened. We may be able to minimize the aftereffects, but we're unable to undo the original incident. Fixating on such events with regret and anger only causes us to hold on to negative emotions regarding them.

Modern stoics practice something they call the "art of acquiescence." It's the acknowledgement that many things lie outside our control and therefore it's better to let them go and move on. They believe this to be the simplest, easiest way to adapt to change.

#18 - Fear of failure

The fear of failure often springs from the same reasons as the pursuit of perfectionism. We entertain this fear because we don't want to let others down. We want to avoid feelings of shame and embarrassment. We don't want our friends, loved ones, and coworkers to think poorly of us.

As you might imagine (or even relate to), this fear immobilizes us. It makes us reluctant to take risks and try new things. This prevents us from enjoying many of the wonderful experiences life offers us.

When we let go of our fear of failure, we become more willing to step outside our comfort zone. Our confidence and self-esteem improve as we take leaps of faith based on the belief that failing doesn't mean disaster. Conversely, our failures often pave the road toward personal growth and self-improvement.

#19 - Others' choices, behaviors, and worldviews

All of us have opinions, and all of us believe we arrived at these opinions through a well-reasoned thought process. We're convinced the facts support our opinions, and thus anyone who harbors conflicting opinions must be wrong. This is a universal attitude. Nearly everyone feels this way.

Problems arise when we allow ourself to become agitated by others' opinions. It's not enough that we feel we're right; we must convince other people that we're right. And so we spend time each day arguing about everything from politics and cultural norms to the economy and whether scrambled eggs should be eaten alone or with ketchup.

Needless to say, this constant bickering can be emotionally exhausting. Moreover, it's rarely rewarding. Letting go of our need to convince others that we're right (in effect, trying to change them) benefits us in several meaningful ways. We begin to prioritize our relationships and improve our connections with other people. We waste less time and energy. And we become more receptive to the possibility that we may be wrong. This, of course, helps us to grow.

#20 - Catastrophic thinking

Some of us fall into a pattern of believing the worst will happen. Not only is this expectation unreasonable, but these worst-case scenarios are often unrealistic. For example, a failed job interview turns into *"I'll never get a job in this industry."* A failed relationship causes us to think *"I'll be alone for the rest of my life."* A child who misses a curfew prompts a catastrophizing parent to fear *"My child must have been terribly injured in a traffic accident."*

Catastrophic thinking stems from a feeling of helplessness. We feel we lack control and influence, and are therefore incapable of resolving issues. So every issue becomes a potential catastrophe, triggering our worst fears.

When we let go of catastrophic thinking, we experience less panic and anxiety. At the same time, our outlook and expectations regarding circumstances that lie beyond our control become more reasonable. This allows us to make better decisions, take more risks, and ultimately enjoy more opportunities with our friends, families, and coworkers.

. . .

THIS CHAPTER WAS A LONG ONE. In fact, it's the longest one you'll find in *The Art of Letting GO*. The upside is that we now have a firm grasp regarding what's at stake. If we can find a way to let go of the 20 things we covered above, our emotional health will improve dramatically.

Keep in mind, we merely scratched the surface in this chapter. There are a myriad of things we should let go, and each of us undoubtedly struggles with unique issues. The good news is, the techniques you'll learn in *Part III* offer universal applicability. You'll be able to use them to resolve nearly *any* type of emotional pain or distress.

Before we get to the tools and strategies in *Part III*, let's explore some of the common reasons we have difficulty letting things go.

PART II

THE MOST COMMON REASONS WE STRUGGLE TO LET GO

~

Deciding to let go of the past is easy. Committing ourself to moving on from our painful memories and negative emotions is simple.

But actually *doing* so is the difficult part.

If a past incident, failed relationship, regrettable decision, or personal grudge bothers us to the point that we obsess over it, our fixation means we consider it important. It doesn't matter whether it truly *is* important to us. We *believe* it to be so. This conviction makes it difficult to let go, no matter how emotionally taxing it is to cling to it.

There are numerous reasons why we resist letting go of the thoughts, emotions, and memories that cause us emotional stress. In this short section, we'll explore those that have the strongest influence on us. You'll recognize some of them immediately. They may even be the cause of your current struggle to let go of a particular issue or grievance. Other reasons may be unfamiliar, and even seem peculiar to you. But you might discover after learning more about them that they too are contributing to your struggle.

Once we recognize *why* our mind resists letting go, we can start the hard (but ultimately rewarding) work of breaking down this resistance. And that's the point at which we can truly begin to abandon our emotional fixation on the past, along with all the pain, stress, and anguish that accompanies it.

Fair warning: we're going to move quickly through this section. We want to gain a full appreciation of why the mind clings to the painful past without getting bogged down in the process. So grab your favorite beverage and get comfortable. I think you'll find the following pages to be both illuminating and sobering.

WE FEAR THE PROSPECT OF CHANGE

> If we don't change, we don't grow. If we don't grow, we aren't really living.

— ANATOLE FRANCE

Change is scary. When we're confronted with it, we fear the uncertainty that accompanies it. Our mind immediately begins to ask questions from a place of concern and anxiety...

- What will this change mean to my life?
- What do I stand to lose as a result?
- Will I be able to adjust to the new circumstances?

- Will I lose control of any aspect of my life?
- Will I be forced to take on more responsibilities?
- Will this change increase the likelihood of my failure?
- Will the new circumstances highlight my deficits and shortcomings?

And so our mind begins to resist. Rather than embrace change, we try to repel it. We prefer the status quo, even if the status quo is a state of misery for us. We're familiar with this state. Although we're unhappy, we fool ourself into thinking we can continue to tolerate it.

When we decide to let go of something, we open ourself to the possibility of living without it. While this change is liberating, we still fear the uncertainty that accompanies it. After all, we've held on to this pain for a long time. We identify with it. It makes us unhappy, but it's familiar to us. Abandoning it is new and scary.

Relinquishing the past encourages us to face this fear. Although doing so makes us feel vulnerable, it's a crucial step toward detaching ourself from the upsetting memories and distressing emotions that burden us.

When we're able to embrace the prospect of change, we can start whittling away at our natural resistance to it. That's when we know we're finally ready to surrender the thing that's been holding us back.

Furthermore, something amazing happens as we continue to embrace change: our confidence grows. Rather than dreading the uncertainty that accompanies change, we start to believe that we can adapt to it. As a result, letting go becomes progressively easier.

WE FEAR THE LOSS OF OPPORTUNITY

 Fear of missing out is the enemy of valuing your own time.

— ANDREW YANG

W e often hold on to negative emotions and unpleasant memories because we dread the possibility that we'll miss out on potential positive experiences associated with them.

For example, we cling emotionally to a failed relationship, refusing to let it go because we hope to somehow salvage it. Or we remain fixated on our decision to abandon a college degree because we hope to one day go back to school to acquire it. Or we dwell on a failed business venture, convinced it failed due to poor timing, and dream of restarting it when the time is right.

This is known as the fear of missing out, or FOMO.

FOMO affects us in many ways. Sometimes, it prevents us from making commitments since doing so limits our options. Other times, it spurs us to constantly check our phones and instinctively say yes to others' offers and invitations. Or we spend money we can't afford because we don't want to miss out on experiences that others are enjoying.

In the context of letting go of the past, FOMO encourages us to remain emotionally attached. If there's even the slightest chance that we can reverse or rectify a regrettable decision or situation, we hold on to that modicum of hope.

We tell ourself that we're simply keeping our options open. But in truth, we're desperately clinging to a desire to "make things right." In doing so, we rob ourself of the opportunity to let go and move on with our life. We prevent ourself from enjoying the personal gratification that accompanies other experiences, relationships, and successes.

The main stumbling block associated with the fear of missing out is found in its name: fear. We fear moving on. We fear missing a chance to experience something good. We fear losing out on something that *might* happen. Unfortunately, this anxiety causes us to perpetuate our suffering by staying emotionally attached to things that make us unhappy.

Several of the tools and techniques we'll cover in *Part*

III will help to counter this mindset and erode the corresponding angst.

WE DREAD LOSING OUR "INVESTMENT"

> 66 The sunk cost fallacy is most dangerous when we have invested a lot of time, money, energy, or love in something. This investment becomes a reason to carry on, even if we are dealing with a lost cause.
>
> — ROLF DOBELLI

All of us have experienced this feeling at some point in our life. We invest so much time, energy, and sometimes money into something that isn't working that we're unable to let it go. We hold on to it despite it making us miserable. Abandoning it and moving on seems impractical given our substantial investment in its success.

This can happen in our professional life as well as our personal life. For example, we stay in a career that makes us unhappy because we invested several years and substantial money toward obtaining a college degree to support it. Or we stay in a toxic relationship because we've invested years of our life and all of our emotional energy in it. We maintain a failing business because we've invested so much time, capital, and even our perception of self-worth into its success.

We don't want to lose our investment. So we hold on, clinging to the thing that's making us feel stressed, anxious, frustrated, bitter, and resentful.

The business world has a term for this mindset: sunk cost fallacy. It describes the inclination to pursue an endeavor because of the resources invested into it, even if those resources cannot be recovered. Additional resources are invested as giving up on the endeavor would mean recognizing its failure.

This idea is just as applicable to our tendency to hold on to things that are causing us emotional discomfort. Letting go of such things means acknowledging that they're not working. And *that* means admitting failure. Admitting failure is always difficult, but doubly so when our sense of self is attached to the thing we're holding on to (a failing relationship, business venture, etc.).

And so we cling to it, sinking additional resources into it. We continue to spend our time, energy, and money on the emotional attachment despite knowing deep down that we'll be unable to recover these resources.

The good news is, once we're able to free ourself from the sunk cost fallacy, it becomes much easier to let things go. We no longer feel beholden to our investment.

WE STRUGGLE WITH LOW SELF-ESTEEM

> No one can make you feel inferior without your consent.

— ELEANOR ROOSEVELT

Low self-esteem discourages us from letting go because we feel that we deserve the regrettable circumstances we've experienced and the resultant emotional pain we're suffering. Rather than recognizing our strengths, we focus on our shortcomings. Instead of celebrating our accomplishments, we castigate ourself for perceived incompetence.

Our headspace is filled with self-recrimination as our inner critic convinces us that we're unlovable, ineffectual, and destined for — and deserving of — failure.

This mindset presses us to hold on to past mistakes, disappointments, and frustrations. We blame ourself for these things. And so we fixate on them, presuming that we "earned" the unhappiness we feel regarding them. Instead of showing ourself compassion, we continue to hold ourself accountable for the past. We refuse to forgive ourself.

For example, recall a past relationship that ended poorly. Numerous factors may have contributed to its failure, including decisions and behaviors by both parties. But if we struggle with low self-esteem, we may assume we're entirely to blame. This assumption, along with the attendant regrets, spurs us to cling to the painful memories rather than letting them go and moving on with our life.

Or suppose we ran a business that went bankrupt. Again, many factors may have played a role in its failure (e.g. bad economy, poor location, increased competition, etc.). If we suffer from low self-esteem, we're likely to blame ourself. Rather than considering the impact of external factors, we'll be inclined to focus on our bad decisions. Instead of looking to the failed business as a learning opportunity, we'll see it as evidence of our ineptitude.

Letting go of the past is only possible if we manage to break this habit of self-reproach. In order to move on, we must find a way to undermine our inner critic, short-circuiting its dubious and emotionally harmful accusations.

Stay with me. The strategies we'll cover in *Part III* are designed to help.

WE LOATHE ADMITTING WE WERE WRONG

" You should never be ashamed to admit you
have been wrong. It only proves you are wiser
today than yesterday.

— JONATHON SWIFT

The unwillingness to admit fault is, in a way, the polar opposite of low self-esteem. Ironically, it has the same effect on our ability to move past painful memories in a healthy manner.

Instead of blaming ourself for unfavorable outcomes, we refuse to acknowledge that we may have played a role. We assume others are entirely at fault. When confronted with evidence that we might share the blame, we go to great lengths to challenge it. Our ego will not allow us to accept blame.

It's easy to assume this mindset would allow us to effortlessly let go of things. After all, if nothing is our fault (at least in our mind), we experience no regret and can therefore move on without a second thought.

Strangely, however, the opposite happens. We experience cognitive dissonance. This is mental stress that occurs when our thoughts, beliefs, decisions, and actions contradict each other. This stress causes us to dwell on our losses and disappointments, dashed expectations, and personal grudges. We continue to blame everyone but ourself, desperately clinging to this narrative rather than simply admitting fault and moving on.

For example, suppose our marriage ends and we refuse to acknowledge that we played a role in its dissolution. We believe we're faultless despite our friends noting that we treated our partner poorly. Cognitive dissonance prevents us from letting the failed marriage go. Instead, the psychological stress causes us to hold on to it, if only to perpetuate the narrative supporting our blamelessness.

Admitting that we're wrong hurts our ego. It tarnishes our self-image. It makes us feel vulnerable and unpleasantly exposed to others' criticism. If we've conditioned ourself to immediately assume we're above reproach and instinctively challenge assertions to the contrary, admitting fault will feel distressing.

But it's a feeling we must overcome. Being able to

admit fault is a necessary step toward letting go of the past and enjoying the emotional freedom and peace of mind that results from moving on.

WE IDEALIZE THE THING WE'RE HANGING ON TO

> My thing is, out of sight, out of mind. That's my attitude toward life. So I don't have any romanticism about any part of my past.
>
> —JOHN LENNON

The entertainment industry has made it more difficult for us to let go of the past. It has *romanticized* the past as well as the idea of holding on to it.

For example, consider novels that focus on the unrequited love of the protagonist. He (or she) yearns for another's affection only to be repeatedly rebuffed or ignored. Rather than accept this circumstance, the protagonist persists in trying to win over the other person. By the end of the book, the protagonist has usually succeeded and everyone lives happily ever after.

Or consider films that focus on a past era (e.g. the 1940s, the Middle Ages, the Renaissance, etc.). Even if the period was marked by violence and bloodshed, it is romanticized by focusing on the hero and his or her journey through various trials and tribulations.

This has had an interesting effect on our psyche. A lifetime of exposure to films, television shows, books, and music that idealize the past has made us more inclined to hold on to things. Rather than letting go of the source of our regrets, disappointments, and painful memories, we sometimes cling to it because we idealize it.

For example, most of us have done this with failed relationships. We hold on to the memories, regardless of the pain they cause, because we idealize former partners and the circumstances we shared with them. We remember the good parts of the relationship while downplaying the bad parts. This is one of the reasons some of us return to toxic relationships. Our idealization of our former partners causes us to forget (or dismiss) the deep-rooted toxicity of the relationship.

We go through this same process with other aspects of the past. For example, we idealize the notion of getting a degree and thus find it difficult to let go of our decision to forgo advanced education. We idealize accomplishing certain goals and thus have trouble letting go of our disappointment at *not* accomplishing them. We idealize being loved by everyone we've known and consequently cling to others' opinions of us, dwelling on their approval or disapproval.

This tendency to idealize the past invariably leads to sadness, frustration, and disappointment. But we can break this habit, giving ourself permission to view our circumstances and our past in a realistic light. When we do so, it becomes much easier to see the past through a pragmatic lens, finally let it go, and ultimately move on with our life.

OUR SELF-IDENTITY IS CONNECTED TO THE THING WE'RE HANGING ON TO

66 When I let go of what I am, I become what I might be. When I let go of what I have, I receive what I need.

— LAO TZU

We self identify with our traumas, triumphs, failures, value systems, vocations, and even material possessions. These things, along with many others, become who we believe ourself to be. We use them as a way to categorize ourself and assign ourself to particular groups.

On the one hand, this practice benefits us. Identifying with things help us to define ourself as individuals. It provides us with a sense of self.

But this practice can also make it more difficult to let things go. When we self identify with particular incidents, circumstances, struggles, belief systems, etc., we become trapped by them. We feel we're unable to leave them behind without leaving an essential part of ourself behind in the process.

For example, suppose you've started several businesses that have ultimately failed. Along the way, you gradually begin to self identify with these business failures. Despite your aspirations, you now secretly think of yourself as an "ineffectual businessperson."

You believe this attribute defines you. You believe it to be a part of your character. Naturally, when you imagine starting another business, this self-imposed label rears its ugly head and immediately discourages you. Worse, you feel as if you'll never be able to break free of it. Like an anchor, it weighs you down.

This occurs whenever we allow our self-identity to become associated with our experiences. A string of failed relationships causes us to believe we're incapable of maintaining a successful one. Being fired from our job makes us feel incompetent at our chosen vocation. Failing to write and publish a novel after years of aspiring to be a career novelist leads us to believe we'll never succeed as one.

These experiences influence how we see ourself. We *become* our failures. Eventually, having connected our self-identity to them, we stop giving ourself the opportunity to succeed.

Abandoning our old identities can be tremendously

liberating. It allows us to more easily let go of awful memories and punishing emotions as we're no longer held captive by demoralizing, self-applied labels.

WE'RE ADDICTED TO NEGATIVE EMOTIONS AND THOUGHTS

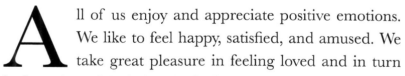 Negative emotions are like unwelcome guests. Just because they show up on our doorstep doesn't mean they have a right to stay.

— DEEPAK CHOPRA

All of us enjoy and appreciate positive emotions. We like to feel happy, satisfied, and amused. We take great pleasure in feeling loved and in turn loving others. We delight in feeling hopeful and awed.

Yet we often focus on negativity. We dwell on painful circumstances. We brood over episodes that cause us to feel anger and resentment. We anguish over disappointments and losses.

Sometimes, we do so purposefully. We ponder negative situations to determine what we did wrong so we can avoid repeating mistakes. But too often, we focus on negativity *without* purpose. We cling to upsetting memories, personal grudges, and judgments about ourself and others. We become addicted to these and other vexing emotions and thoughts.

It's counterintuitive, to be sure. Why would any of us *choose* to fixate on anger, sadness, and fear when we instinctively enjoy feeling calm, happy, and secure?

Psychologists claim it can be a form of emotional addiction, one that stems from a variety of sources. One possible reason is feeling unable to control our circumstances. Another is that we're trying to make sense of something (an incident, outcome, etc.) that seems nonsensical to us. Yet another reason is to reassure ourself that our decisions and actions in a particular situation were correct. Essentially, that we are blameless for whatever caused us to experience the negative emotions in the first place.

Whatever the reason (or reasons) for this fixation, it impedes our ability to let go and move on. When we obsess about an unfortunate incident, disappointed expectations, or anything that causes us to feel frustrated, angry, offended, or resentful, we condition our mind to hold on to the negative emotions associated with them. This conditioning encourages us to attach ourself to them rather than surrendering them.

This behavior can become so ingrained that it happens without our realizing it. And we end up holding on to things even though they caused — and *continue* to cause — us emotional distress.

OUR BRAINS ARE HARDWIRED TO SURVIVE

66 Bad things happen. And the human brain is especially adept at making sure that we keep track of these events. This is an adaptive mechanism important for survival.

— DAVID PERLMUTTER

The mind prioritizes survival above all other concerns. It is designed to help us overcome dangerous situations and evade threats and hazards to our well-being. This priority to survive is paramount and unseats all other competing interests. It's a part of our natural programming; this biological imperative is hardwired into us.

One of the primary ways in which the brain prioritizes

survival is by recognizing and storing negative information. It remembers experiences that caused us harm, both physically and psychologically. In doing so, it helps us to avoid or pull through circumstances that jeopardize our comfort and security.

The mind's tendency to focus on the negative (psychologists call this tendency "negativity bias") helped our ancestors to survive environmental dangers. It allowed them to stay alert to threatening conditions when a single error in judgment might otherwise have disastrous consequences.

This negativity bias clearly has its uses. But today, its psychological impact arguably outweighs them. First, we are less exposed to environmental dangers than were our ancestors. Threats still exist, of course. But our vulnerability to them has greatly diminished.

Second, while focusing on the negative, the mind tends to overlook the positive. Because the latter *seems* to have minimal practical use, it is disregarded.

Third, this negativity bias discourages us from letting go of negative thoughts and emotions. Our mind, prioritizing our survival, overemphasizes their usefulness. We hold on to them, intuitively presuming that doing so protects us from future harm. This tendency impacts every area of our life, from our relationships and careers to our ability to make good, reasoned decisions when we're confronted with competing options.

Overcoming this natural proclivity toward the negative requires that we rewire our brain. We must reframe negative experiences of the past in order to finally let them go. Additionally, we must create new ways to think about our circumstances so that we entertain negative aspects only to the extent of their practical usefulness.

The strategies and exercises we'll cover in *Part III* will prove instrumental to these ends.

PART III

21 STRATEGIES FOR LETTING GO AND MOVING ON WITH YOUR LIFE

~

We've set the stage. We've laid the foundation. Now it's time for us to do the work. This section of *The Art of Letting GO* is where the rubber meets the road. The pages that follow are filled with *actionable* tips and tools that can be put to use immediately.

We're going to explore, step by step, an assortment of techniques. These techniques will help us to evaluate painful memories and undo the anger, resentment, disappointments, judgments, and personal grudges that are currently holding us back.

This isn't just about self-evaluation. We're going to venture much further. Our end goal is to reverse years of conditioning that are causing us to needlessly hold on to toxic relationships, regrettable decisions, grievous losses, and bitterness over shattered expectations.

The strategies we'll cover will help us to override our mental pattern of regret, guilt, and self-recrimination regarding things we can't change. They'll allow us to gradually replace our feelings of remorse, shame, and general discontent with self-compassion. These techniques will encourage us to develop a mindset that emphasizes self-empathy, patience, and forgiveness.

Ultimately, they'll help us to gather the courage we need to finally let go of the things that are causing us to feel miserable and dejected. And once we're able to do so, we'll finally be able to move on and create the life we deserve.

One quick reminder: each of the sections that follow contains an exercise. These exercises are simple and designed to be performed quickly. But don't underestimate them. They provide an opportunity to put the concepts we'll explore to use, turning advice into action.

Ready to stop feeling trapped by the past and present and experience true emotional relief and freedom going forward? If so, let's roll up our sleeves and get to work.

STRATEGY #1: MAKE THE DECISION TO LET GO

66 Yesterday is not ours to recover, but tomorrow is ours to win or lose.

— LYNDON B. JOHNSON

~

We want to make positive changes in our life. We desire these changes for a variety of reasons. Sometimes, it's because they'll help us to become a better, kinder, more reliable friend, spouse, or coworker. Other times, we want them because we believe they'll improve our quality of life.

The most important thing to keep in mind is that *wanting* to make a positive change isn't the same as *deciding* to make it. The former is little more than wish fulfillment.

The latter is a commitment, a decision that is far more likely to result in the change we desire.

Making the decision to let go of something is more complicated than it sounds. First, we need to acknowledge the source of our unhappiness. We must ask ourself *"What is causing my emotional pain?"*

Second, we need to determine whether we're ready to commit to letting go of this burden. Here, we need motivation to spur our commitment. Let's ask ourself *"How will my life improve once I'm free of this painful memory, regret, or frustration?"*

Third, we must identify the potential reasons our mind might resist letting go of this emotional albatross. Do we identify with the pain? Are we struggling with low self-esteem and thus believe we're unworthy of forgiveness and happiness? Review the common reasons we covered in *Part II*. It's highly likely that at least one of them applies here.

Fourth, we must recognize that the decision to let go is ultimately ours to make. No one else can make this decision for us. Recognizing this gives us a sense of purpose. It encourages us to acknowledge our agency in our life.

As an example, suppose you're finding it difficult to let go of a failed relationship. First, identify the source of your unhappiness. Perhaps it's a fateful decision you made that doomed the relationship. Maybe it's verbal abuse on the part of your partner.

Next, consider how your life will improve once you decide to let go of this pain. You'll feel less burdened.

You'll have more confidence in yourself. You'll feel more optimistic about life's possibilities.

Then, determine why you're holding on to the relationship. Is low self-esteem preventing you from seeking a healthier relationship (i.e. you don't believe you deserve it)? Or perhaps you dread confronting the fact that you suspected the relationship was doomed from the beginning, and nevertheless pursued it.

Lastly, accept that the decision to let go of the failed relationship is yours to make. You have agency. You have the capacity to make this decision.

∼

EXERCISE #1

∼

WRITE a statement that summarizes your decision to let go of the event, decision, relationship, or memory that's causing you misery. Post it somewhere in plain sight (above your desk, on your refrigerator, etc.). This statement should incorporate the four steps above.

Here's an example:

- "I'm committing to finally let go of
  _____.

- By letting _____ go, I'll feel less stressed and less discouraged. I'll also feel better about myself with great self-confidence and a more positive outlook regarding my potential.

- It's possible my mind might resist. After all, I've been holding on to _____ for years. I identify with the pain. I also idealize _____ despite knowing the ideal is impossible.
- I alone have the power to make this decision. I alone get to decide to let go of

_____.

Time required: 10 minutes

STRATEGY #2: IDENTIFY YOUR EMOTIONAL STATE

> You cannot let go of anything if you cannot notice that you are holding it. Admit your 'weaknesses' and watch them morph into your greatest strengths.
>
> — NEALE DONALD WALSCH

Before we can let go of something, we need to know how it's affecting our emotions. It's one thing to feel a particular emotion, such as anger, guilt, or sadness. But it's another thing entirely to understand how it's impacting our frame of mind and influencing the way we feel about ourself and everything around us.

For example, suppose we're feeling angry about a failed

relationship. This anger doesn't exist in a vacuum. It causes a ripple effect that extends to other areas of our life. It makes us irritable at our workplace. It make us temperamental when we're with our friends. It causes us to be impatient when we interact with strangers.

It's important that we understand how the troubling emotions we experience affect our broader emotional state. How do they influence our interpretation of our circumstances? How do they affect the manner in which — and the effectiveness with which — we approach challenges and solve problems? How do they govern our worldview and prejudice our perspective?

Simply put, we often underestimate the emotions we feel regarding a particular incident, decision, or memory. We know we feel them. But we overlook how they influence our headspace.

The ability to comprehend, evaluate, and manage our emotional state is known as emotional intelligence (EQ). It involves deep introspection into how we're feeling, why we're feeling this way, how these feelings are affecting us, and whether we need to take action to manage them.

This process requires self-awareness. We need to be able to observe how we're feeling and figure out whether these feelings make sense. We need to investigate how the emotions that stem from a particular memory or grievance exert influence on our reactions, impulses, and behaviors in other areas of our life.

The first step toward doing this is to find a quiet place to sit and think. This space should be free of distractions (e.g. our phones, the television, other people, etc.).

Second, we should ask ourself a simple, two-pronged question: *"What am I feeling and what is causing me to feel this way?"*

Third, we reflect on how these emotions are affecting our behaviors — at our workplace, with our friends, with our loved ones, and even when we're alone.

Fourth, we write everything down.

As we go through this process, we may feel guilty about our emotions. We may feel ashamed regarding how they influence us. It's crucial that we resist the urge to criticize ourself for feeling the way we do. Otherwise, we risk instinctively suppressing these unpleasant emotions. This would prevent us from evaluating, managing, and resolving them.

∼

EXERCISE #2

∼

FIND a quiet space free of distractions. Take a pen and pad of paper with you.

Think about a recent incident or circumstance that made you feel angry or sad. Describe the incident in a single sentence. For example, *"I got stuck in traffic on my way home from the office."* Write it down.

Next, list the emotions you experienced during and after the incident. Anger? Frustration? Scorn? Write them down.

Now, describe how these emotions affected your behavior immediately following the incident. Use short sentences. For example, *"I snapped at my spouse"* or *"I slammed the door when I got home."* Write these down.

Finally, read what you've written and ponder how the emotions you felt affected your behaviors and reactions in situations unrelated to the incident.

Time required: 10 minutes

STRATEGY #3: FIND AN OUTLET FOR YOUR NEGATIVE EMOTIONS

66 Hanging onto resentment is letting someone you despise live rent-free in your head.

— ANN LANDERS

Letting go of a painful memory, bitter grudge, regrettable decision, or grief and sadness stemming from a personal loss is easier when we have an outlet for these emotions. Having an outlet doesn't *resolve* the emotions. But it gives us a way to release some of the stress and anxiety they create so that they don't overwhelm us. That's important. We're better able to evaluate our emotional state in the absence of such pressure.

Many people find emotional solace in physical activity.

They visit the gym. They participate in sports. They clean their house. They go for a run.

Others find comfort in talking to friends. This might include expressing their emotional struggles. Or it can simply be spending time with people they love and admire.

Still others find relaxing activities, such as reading, meditating, or painting, ease their stress and provide succor.

Think about the activities you enjoy. Consider how they make you feel. For example, does people-watching at a local park or mall relax you? Does watching a cheesy romantic comedy make you feel happy? Does spending time with a close friend cause you to feel inspired and grateful for the friendship?

Each of these can offer a valuable outlet for your negative emotions. The key is to *do* them.

When we feel miserable about something we're having difficulty letting go, it's common to isolate ourself and wallow in our misery. Our brain fixates on the source of our emotional pain, and other activities get sidelined by this fixation. We can't imagine doing something that gives us joy while we feel this way.

This is the moment when we should force ourself to take advantage of activities we enjoy. We may not *feel* like visiting the park to people-watch, but this is precisely what we *should* do when we're feeling miserable (if that's what relaxes us). We may not *feel* like watching a cheesy romantic comedy, but we should do exactly that.

Forcing ourself to do things we enjoy short circuits the

pattern of negative thoughts and emotions that dominate our headspace. It provides a useful and timely outlet for the attendant stress. Releasing this stress will help us to confront the thing we're holding on to with less emotional attachment and greater purpose.

∾

EXERCISE #3

∾

IDENTIFY five activities that make you feel good. They should be reliable and consistent. They make you feel happy, relaxed, satisfied, or inspired every time you do them.

Make certain they're simple and easy. That way you can do them whenever you wish with minimal planning or expenditure. Examples include walking your dog, reading a novel, and visiting a local park, museum, or coffeeshop.

Write down these five activities. Post the list in a place where they're always visible. Posting this list eases the burden of having to remember these activities when your mind is saddled with distressing emotions.

The next time you find yourself in anguish over something, immediately refer to this list and force yourself to do one of the activities.

Time required: 5 minutes

STRATEGY #4: DETERMINE WHETHER YOUR NEEDS ARE BEING MET

> All moralistic judgments, whether positive or negative, are tragic expressions of unmet needs.

— MARSHALL ROSENBERG

It's hard to feel happy when our needs aren't being met. We feel dissatisfied. It's as if a cloud of discontent follows us wherever we go. We know intuitively that we're not experiencing something essential to our happiness, even if we're unable to precisely identify what that something is.

When we have difficulty letting go of something, it's often because we believe it was meeting one of our needs. For example, a failed relationship was providing love and companionship. A failed business was providing a sense of accomplishment, which in turn boosted our self-confidence. Others' expectations gave us a sense of personal value.

This perception is often misguided (which we'll get to in a moment), but we *believe* it to be true. Until we recognize and acknowledge the delusion, it may as well be true. Ultimately, it makes us less inclined to let go of whatever is burdening us.

The irony is, this misperception not only sabotages our ability to let go, but also prevents us from getting our needs actually met. For example, we hold on to a toxic relationship because it makes us feel secure. But the feeling is a mirage due to the relationship's toxicity. Holding on to it means we miss the opportunity to enjoy a *healthy* relationship that would allow us to experience genuine emotional security.

For this reason, in order to let something go, we need to determine whether it's truly meeting our needs. The first step is figuring out what our needs are.

Maslow's hierarchy of needs[1] is helpful in this regard, but we need to explore further to fully understand our personal motivations. For example, knowing that we need to experience "self-actualization" to feel motivated is only useful to a limited extent. What does it mean to us on a *personal* level?

First, we need to ask ourself *"what do I need in order to feel satisfied?"* Love and affection? Self-confidence? A sense of independence? Frequent opportunities to show empathy toward others? It's important to be specific. The next step depends on it.

Second, we need to determine whether the thing we're holding on to truly meets any of these needs. This requires careful thought and introspection. It's possible that we've been misinterpreting the signals (perhaps for years), mistakenly believing that our needs are being met when in reality they're not.

Once we're able to recognize that the thing we're clinging to isn't meeting any of our needs, we can more easily sever our attachment to it. We can let it go and finally move on.

∿

EXERCISE #4

∿

FIND a quiet space and contemplate your personal needs. Ask yourself what you need in order to feel satisfied. Write down everything that comes to mind.

Your needs might involve your connections with other people (affection, companionship, etc.). Perhaps they include a sense of safety and security (structure, predictability, etc.). Maybe you need opportunities to experience adventure, passion, and spontaneity. Or you may need to feel productive, effective, and highly competent in your areas of expertise.

If you've never done this exercise, you may be surprised by the results. It's one thing to know instinctively what you need in order to feel happy and fulfilled. It's another thing entirely to see your needs written down in front of you.

Now that you've written down your needs, scrutinize every toxic relationship, unfortunate decision, or personal grievance you're holding on to in light of them. Audit them one by one, asking yourself *"does this thing actually meet any of the needs I've identified?"*

If the answer is "no" (and it likely will be), it becomes much easier to recognize its uselessness and the futility of holding on to it.

Time required: 30 minutes

---

1. https://en.wikipedia.org/wiki/Maslow%27s_hierarchy_of_needs

STRATEGY #5: IDENTIFY WHAT GIVES YOUR LIFE PURPOSE

> 66 The mystery of human existence lies not in just staying alive, but in finding something to live for.

— FYODOR DOSTOYEVSKY

This strategy is a cousin to Strategy #4. In the previous section, we focused on determining whether our painful memories and negative emotions stem from something that truly met our needs — or merely *seemed* to meet them. In this section, we'll dig one level deeper. We'll investigate whether the thing we're holding on to gives our life purpose.

Purpose motivates us. It fills us with resolve and encourages us to take action. It influences our behaviors and helps us to make difficult decisions. It aids us in regulating our emotions and allows us to focus on what matters to us. Purpose gives our life meaning and plays a critical role in whether we feel fulfilled or dissatisfied.

When we're clear about our purpose, we're optimistic. We recognize that life has a lot to offer and want to take advantage of opportunities to enjoy it. We know what we're supposed to do, or are at least confident that we can figure it out.

By contrast, when we don't know what gives us purpose, we feel bored, empty, and anxious. We might even feel hopeless, a sentiment that reinforces the false and damaging internal narrative that we lack personal agency.

This lack of awareness regarding our purpose makes us more inclined to hold on to the past. The future seems arbitrary and pointless, which makes the past seem more important to us.

For this reason, identifying what gives us purpose is an essential part of letting go. Once we determine that an upsetting memory, distressing incident, or lamentable decision is disconnected from the things that give our life purpose, it appears less impactful to us. And that shift in perspective makes the process of letting it go much easier.

So how do we identify what gives our life purpose? As you can imagine, introspection plays a key role. We need to ask probing questions that help us to determine what we find truly meaningful. These questions will gradually reveal the aspects of life we value. These can range from social connections and professional success to personal development and spirituality.

We'll explore these questions in the exercise below.

One quick note: what gives us purpose today may be different tomorrow. That's fine. In fact, it's to be expected. We evolve. Sometimes, we reinvent ourself to align with new circumstances and aspirations. So the exercise that follows is worth repeating from time to time.

∾

EXERCISE #5

∾

By now, you know the drill: Grab a pen and pad of paper, and find a quiet space that's free of distractions.

Let's start with a couple of general questions. The questions will become more specific and probing as we move forward. Write down each one, and leave a bit of space for your answers.

Question #1: *"What makes me happy?"*

Forget about things you feel that you must do or feel deserve your attention. Ignore things you do to impress others or maintain an image. Just think about what makes you happy.

Question #2: "*What moves me?*"

Consider things that grab your attention and evoke an emotional response. These are things about which you're passionate. It's likely they align with your values.

Question #3: "*What am I good at?*"

Whether your expertise stems from innate talent or years of education and practice, these are things that *feel* effortless. You do them well, and you do them with ease.

Question #4: "*What are my biggest fears?*"

These fears hold you back from pursuing the things that give you purpose. Perhaps it's a fear of failure. Maybe it's a fear of success. Or maybe it's a fear of being judged by others.

Question #5: "*If I knew I was going to pass away in five years, how would I spend my remaining time?*"

It's a morbid question, to be sure. But it's also a useful one. It encourages us to consider what we feel is truly important. With limited time at our disposal, we're compelled to devote it to pursuits and interests that we feel are meaningful.

Question #6: "*Who would I like to be 10 years from today?*"

Here, we consider the goals we aspire to accomplish and the reasons we want to accomplish them. We think about the possessions we want to acquire and the reasons we want to acquire them. We contemplate the type of friend, parent, sibling, or coworker we want to be and why we want to be so. In short, this question encourages us to ponder our future identity along with our motives.

Question #7: *"If I look back on my life near its end, how would I imagine having lived it successfully?"*

Our life near its end will no doubt look much differently than it does today. We'll have the advantage of hindsight. This question helps us to preemptively reflect on our life. Did we live it according to our values and priorities? Did we make the contributions we aspire to make? Did we make a difference in a way that's meaningful to us?

Mulling over and candidly answering these questions allows us to brush aside life's trivial concerns and focus on what actually matters to us. It clarifies what gives us purpose. It encourages our intentionality. In the process, it sheds light on our troubling memories and bleak thoughts, urging us to accept they may be pointless and thus suitable to let go.

Time required: 30 minutes

STRATEGY #6: ACKNOWLEDGE YOUR EMOTIONAL PAIN

> 66 As long as you are unable to access the power of the Now, every emotional pain that you experience leaves behind a residue of pain that lives on in you.
>
> — ECKHART TOLLE

Many of us avoid emotional pain. We distract ourself from it by focusing on our work, buying things we don't need, and even indulging in behavior we know to be self-destructive (binge drinking, drug use, self-injury, etc.). In short, we go to great lengths to keep the pain at bay.

But in order to let go of the pain, we have to confront it

head on. We have to face it without distraction. Only then can we release it, grieve when necessary, and move on with our life.

Emotional pain can stem from a myriad of circumstances. A shattered relationship, the loss of a loved one, and persistent social isolation can cause us to suffer anguish and distress. Low self-esteem, the loss of a job, and mistreatment by coworkers can have the same effect.

When we experience mental suffering, we sometimes respond to it by shutting off our emotions. We stoically deal with the pain by bottling it up and getting on with life. Unfortunately, this approach prevents us from properly dealing with it and managing the emotions it evokes in us. We rob ourself of the opportunity to express and release the negative feelings we experience.

And this makes letting go practically impossible.

Rather than avoid our emotional misery, we must embrace it. We should be willing to admit we're feeling the way we feel, accept it as authentic and valid, and let it in. This process isn't about giving ourself approval to feel like a victim. Instead, its purpose is to acknowledge our distress rather than bottling it up, identify its source, confront it head-on, and ultimately free ourself from it.

This is how we let it go, heal, forgive, repair our self-worth, and move on.

The exercise below is designed to help us to go through this process. It's simple and easy. But don't rush through it. Give yourself time to fully appreciate the pain you're feeling regarding the thing you're holding on to.

~

EXERCISE #6

~

FIRST, start a journal. In this journal write down what you're feeling.

Be as specific as possible. Do you feel sad, angry, traumatized, or powerless? Do you feel lonely, empty inside, depressed, or overwhelmed? Write down every emotion you're experiencing. This entry in your journal doesn't need to be long or eloquent. A simply bullet-point list will suffice.

Next, set your journal aside, close your eyes, and identify the event, circumstance, or source of these feelings. What is making you feel the way you feel? Once you've identified the source, open your eyes and retrieve your journal. Describe the origin of your emotional pain. Be concise. One or two sentences should be adequate.

Lastly, start an entry in the format of a brief letter to yourself. In this letter, explain what happened and how it made you feel. You've already done most of the work. Refer to what you've already written down.

Writing this letter gives you an opportunity to acknowledge your pain and express your feelings. It makes them more tangible and palpable. This, in turn, makes it easier to accept what you're feeling as authentic, embrace the pain, and understand why you're feeling it.

Time required: 15 minutes

STRATEGY #7: LOOK FOR IMPORTANT LESSONS

 In the process of letting go you will lose many things from the past, but you will find yourself.

— DEEPAK CHOPRA

All of us have regrets. We make mistakes. We make poor choices. We say things we wish we hadn't. We knowingly engage in activities detrimental to our physical and mental health. We fail to take advantage of opportunities. Regrets are an inescapable part of life.

But this doesn't mean we need to hold on to them. In fact, holding on to a regret often suggests we haven't learned anything from it. We haven't discerned its lesson.

Yet.

Our mistakes present terrific learning opportunities. When we're willing to examine them, they help us to identify our activities, behaviors, and decisions that resulted in undesirable outcomes.

Examining our regrets, looking for any lessons they offer us, is often the key to letting them go. If we can take away from them some insight that helps us to act, behave, or decide more effectively in the future, they'll have served a useful purpose. Discovering this insight can feel invigorating.

Rather than feeling discouraged and depressed, the lessons we learn make us feel more optimistic. We experience a greater sense of confidence and agency. Instead of continually thinking "life stinks," we imagine the positive changes we can make thanks to our improved awareness.

This requires a shift in our mindset. Previously, we fixated on our painful memories, pessimistic thoughts, disappointments and dashed expectations, and various grudges and grievances. We felt unable to detach ourself from them. They burdened us, weighing us down and preventing us from experiencing the happiness and joy that accompany emotional freedom.

Now, in shifting our mindset, we proactively search for teachable moments. We look for lessons in our misfortune, sorrow, and distress through which we can grow.

This shift isn't easy. Far from it, in fact. Most of us have to confront and negate years of conditioning to make it happen. But like any new habit, we can do so through repeated application. If we train ourself to consistently look for enlightenment in things that evoke our negative emotions, the practice will eventually become second nature to us.

This makes letting go of the regrets and negativity attached to these things much easier.

∿

EXERCISE #7

∿

THINK about something you're struggling to let go. Maybe it's a shattered relationship, botched presentation for your job, or a decision that caused you to lose a substantial amount of money. Perhaps it's a behavior you loathe in yourself, but continue to engage in (e.g. procrastinating, trying to please others, breaking promises, etc.).

Whatever it is, write it down.

Next, write down this question: *"Why do I feel regret over this?"* Answer it candidly. Does your regret or remorse stem from something you did? If so, what was it?

This question serves two purposes. First, it helps us to separate things we have control over from those we don't. If we lack control, there's no reason to blame ourself.

Second, if we *did* have control, it encourages us to own the mistake. This is a crucial step toward learning from it.

Next, write down this question: *"What was I trying to accomplish?"* Again, answer it candidly. The action, behavior, or decision clearly failed to meet our expectations. This question highlights what went wrong.

Finally, write down this question: "*What can I learn from this experience?*" The purpose of this question is to help us avoid making the same error in the future. If we had control and did something we now regret, we can gain useful insight from the experience. With it, we can make positive changes.

This exercise encourages us to make use of uncomfortable memories, losses and disappointments, and unpleasant episodes rather than remain burdened by them. Putting their lessons into practice reinforces our sense of agency and makes it easier for us to let them go.

Time required: 15 minutes

STRATEGY #8: RECOGNIZE THAT YOUR IDEAL SELF IS A MIRAGE

 Embrace the glorious mess that you are.

— ELIZABETH GILBERT

We aspire to be better. We have an image of the person we'd like to be in the future and strive to make that image a reality. That's part of the human condition. It's an honorable intention and plays an important role in our continual growth.

But it's a double-edged sword. Our intention to be better is accompanied by the awareness that we're not currently the person we believe we should be. Our present self has fallen short of our ideal self in some way.

For example, suppose we've always imagined becoming a surgeon. We attend medical school, obtain our degree, and go through a medical residency program only to discover we can't stand the sight of blood. Suddenly our ideal self is in jeopardy. Our present, *real* self has fallen short of our idealized image.

This sets the stage for pointless self-criticism. We castigate ourself because we believe we've failed to "measure up." We think of our failed expectations and the attendant lost opportunities, which fills us with regret, bitterness, and disappointment.

These feelings, left unchallenged, gain their own momentum. They can eventually dominate our headspace, causing us to obsess over our perceived failure to actualize our ideal self. This frame of mind traps us in a state of remorse and shame. We become fixated on things that "should have been" rather than accepting the present, surrendering what we can't control, and moving on.

With this unhealthy, self-punishing attitude in place, letting go becomes impossible.

It's imperative that we recognize that our idealized self is little more than a mirage. It's an unattainable illusion, much like the proverbial oasis in a desert. As long as we cling to the fantasy, we prevent ourself from coming to terms with our *real* self. We forego the opportunity to reconcile our current circumstances and let go of our painful memories, dashed expectations, and disappointments regarding what we believe should have been.

Surrendering our ideal self is a process, not merely a decision. It requires giving attention to — and adjusting —

certain aspects of our current frame of mind. The following exercise is designed to help.

~

EXERCISE #8

~

GRAB your pen and pad of paper. Write down the heading *"My Values"* and list every personal value you consider to be important.

Your list may include things like loyalty, spirituality, and security. It might include courage, compassion, and honesty. Perhaps you value self-reliance, determination, and a strong work ethic. Whatever it is, write it down. Make the list as comprehensive as possible.

Next, underneath your list of values, write down the heading *"My Interests."* List everything you feel passionate about.

Consider your favorite hobbies, such as cooking, gardening, or playing the guitar. Think about things you find intriguing, such as reading about history, following select social causes, or traveling to faraway countries.

Lastly, underneath your list of interests, write down the heading *"Areas That Deserve More of My Time."* Write down values you currently hold dear that you feel need more attention. List your interests and passions that you've placed on the back burner.

This exercise encourages us to focus on our *present* self rather than fixating on our *ideal* self. Instead of aspiring to measure up to an unattainable, idealized image of ourself, we recognize our current circumstances and simply strive to improve. Along the way, we feel empowered to let go of our regrets and disappointments over the person we thought we should have been.

Time required: 20 minutes

STRATEGY #9: SURRENDER YOUR PRIDE

66 Pride costs us more than hunger, thirst, and cold.

— THOMAS JEFFERSON

We sometimes mistake pride for self-esteem and self-confidence. For example, we're "proud" of ourself for having gone to school and received a degree in our chosen field of study. We're "proud" of ourself for maintaining a healthy marriage. We're "proud" of ourself for running a successful business.

But pride flirts with the dark side of our ego. Left unchecked, it can cause us to feel arrogant and self-important. When it does so, it becomes a destructive force. It turns into a stumbling block that negatively impacts our relationships, careers, and decisions.

Unchallenged, pride also discourages us from letting go the things that haunt us. We become less inclined to admit our mistakes, convinced we're faultless. We become less willing to apologize, certain that others are to blame and thus owe *us* an apology. We habitually compare ourself to others to measure our self-worth, and obsess over keeping up with them.

These tendencies erode our ability and willingness to let go of grievances, judgments, personal grudges, and other sources of bitterness, resentment, and emotional distress. Instead, we cling to these things. They allow us to feel superior to others, a sentiment that we convince ourself is essential to our positive self-image.

To be clear, pride isn't inherently bad. In fact, it serves a useful purpose. It encourages us to appreciate our strengths, and it inspires us to accomplish goals that are important to us. But like our aspiration to be better, it's a double-edge sword. It courts egotism and narcissism. When we're overly prideful, we become so intent on presenting a superior image that we're unable to let go of anything that challenges it, privately or publicly.

For this reason, we must be willing to surrender our pride. By doing so, we remove one of the most paralyzing roadblocks hampering our ability to let go the things that cause us emotional turmoil.

To be clear, surrendering our pride doesn't mean that we abandon our self-respect. Rather, we simply recognize our fallibility. We continue to appreciate our strengths and values while acknowledging that we're human and thus capable of doing things, saying things, and feeling things that are detrimental to us.

So how do we ensure that pride doesn't take over our life? How do we manage it so that it doesn't hamper our ability to let go of the things that make us miserable?

Grab your pen and pad of paper for Exercise #9.

∼

EXERCISE #9

∼

First, write down the heading *"Things for Which I'm Proud of Myself."* Underneath it, list everything that gives you a sense of personal pride. Include goals you've achieved, lessons you've learned, and personal struggles you've overcome.

Perhaps you were offered a coveted job after a successful interview. Maybe you learned how to cook a difficult dish. Perhaps you went on a date that went fantastically well. Write it down. Take time to make the list exhaustive. The more comprehensive it is, the better.

Next, write down the heading *"Things That Made Me Feel Defensive."* List every recent circumstance during which you found yourself justifying your actions, behaviors, decisions, and even private thoughts.

Perhaps you argued with a coworker, and he claimed that your actions caused a problem. Maybe a friend offered you constructive criticism about a recent investment decision. Perhaps a neighbor purchased a new car and you found yourself privately rationalizing why you drive an older vehicle. Again, the more comprehensive you make this list, the better.

Lastly, consider each item that you've placed on your second list. One by one, ask yourself *"does this contradict any item I've placed on my first list?"* For example, does your neighbor purchasing a new car invalidate the fact that you got a coveted job? Does it invalidate the fact that you learned to cook a difficult dish?

You'll find that your answer in every case will almost certainly be *"no"* or even *"of course not."*

Going through this process serves an important purpose. It severs the connection between the things that give you a legitimate sense of confidence and the things that spur you to reactively protect your ego. Along the way, it'll become easier and more natural to admit mistakes, accept culpability, and forego making trivial and useless comparisons with others.

And *that* will make letting go much simpler.

Time required: 30 minutes

STRATEGY #10: ACKNOWLEDGE THE DEBILITATING EFFECTS OF GUILT AND SHAME

> Shame corrodes the very part of us that believes we are capable of change.
>
> — BRENE BROWN

Guilt and shame are painful, crippling emotions. Both are reminders that we've done something wrong, often producing terrible consequences, for ourself and others, in the process. These emotions can make us feel innately flawed, contemptible, and morally deficient. They can make us feel unworthy of others' affection and companionship. Left unresolved, they can cause us intense stress and anxiety and trap us in a state of perpetual self-reproach.

But like pride (discussed in the previous chapter), both

guilt and shame serve a useful, if unpleasant, purpose. They signal to our brain that our behavior and conduct are misaligned with our values. They highlight our moral and ethical failings as we perceive them in light of our principles.

When we're mindful of our emotions, we can make use of guilt and shame to change our behavior. We can examine our misdeed, determine why it caused us to feel guilt and shame, and self-correct. We can realign our conduct with our values.

Unfortunately, many of us seldom reach this stage. We fail to take the time to fully reflect upon our emotions and investigate their source, and thus allow guilt and shame to fester in our mind. We realize we did something that makes us feel terrible, but avoid reconciling this feeling due to ego, pride, and fear. This allows our always-present inner critic to turn into a voice of condemnation.

Over time, this self-criticism can destroy our self-image and demolish our self-esteem. It gains a foothold in our brain. Once this happens, it becomes more difficult to show ourself compassion and forgiveness. We continue to punish ourself for our perceived misdeeds rather than confronting the guilt and shame they evoke and letting them go.

This state of mind eventually hobbles our ability to act with confidence and purpose. And it impacts every area of our life. Unable (or unwilling) to forgive ourself, we become stuck in the past and unable to move forward.

The first step toward letting go of our guilt and shame

is to recognize how they negatively impact our life. This is more complicated than it sounds and requires a fair bit of self-analysis. The following exercise will guide you through the process.

∼

EXERCISE #10

∼

WRITE down something you recently did that made you feel guilty and ashamed. Describe the circumstance and recount your thought process. What prompted you to do what you did? No one will read what you write (unless you allow them), so be candid.

Next, write down the reason (or reasons) your conduct caused you to feel guilty and ashamed. Did your behavior violate a particular value that you normally embrace? If so, write down that value. If your behavior transgressed more than one, write down all of them.

Now, describe the emotions you're experiencing associated with your guilt and shame stemming from this incident. Express them thoroughly. For example, you may be fearful of condemnation from someone you wronged. Or perhaps you feel deeply embarrassed by your conduct. Or maybe you feel that your behavior was so reprehensible that you're unworthy of forgiveness, from yourself and others.

Lastly, focus on each of these feelings, one by one, and consider their effects on your future actions and decisions. For example, fear of condemnation from someone you've wronged may cause you to avoid that individual, amplifying your guilt and shame. Profound embarrassment might discourage you from associating with others, leading to isolation and despair. Feeling unworthy of forgiveness may prompt you to denigrate every thought you have, leading to emotional paralysis.

As you've likely noticed, this exercise doesn't focus on letting go of our guilt and shame. That comes later. Rather, it focuses exclusively on their negative impacts. That's the critical first step, and it's one that sorely deserves our time and attention.

By taking this step (i.e. doing this exercise), we're better able to recognize how guilt and shame undermine our ability to act, forgive, and ultimately heal and recover.

Time required: 20 minutes

STRATEGY #11: DISREGARD WHAT OTHERS THINK OF YOU

> Care about what other people think and you will always be their prisoner.
>
> — LAO TZU

We care what others think of us. It's instinctive. Much of our happiness stems from the relationships we enjoy with other people. Naturally, we want them to like, respect, and admire us. We model our behavior and decisions to ensure this effect. We do things we know will elicit a positive response from our friends, coworkers, loved ones, and even acquaintances. Conversely, we *avoid* doing things we suspect would evoke a negative response.

This instinct can be beneficial to us. It encourages us to

maintain certain behavioral standards, pressuring us to *help* others rather than hurt them (deliberately or otherwise). This impulse was vital to our survival back when our ancestors had to contend with predators, environmental hazards, and other threats. If we behaved to the detriment of the group, we might be ostracized and left behind. And then we'd find ourself in big trouble.

But like pride, this instinct is a double-edged sword. And it can easily cut both ways.

Today, we don't have to contend with the hazards and threats that endangered our ancestors. Our life is rarely in immediate peril. So group inclusion is no longer a matter of survival.

Still, we continue to strive for others' approval. We worry constantly about what others think of us. We dread criticism and model our behavior and decisions to avoid it. In short, we still fear being rejected and excluded from the group.

The problem is, this fear makes it nearly impossible for us to let go of things that cause us emotional pain and distress. When we obsess over receiving others' approval, we give ourself far less latitude to confront our emotions, forgive ourself, and move on. The process of letting go becomes entangled with our yearning for others' validation. Our insecurity causes us to overanalyze our thoughts, decisions, and actions under the harsh, unforgiving light of whether we have others' permission.

We need to break this cycle. We need to abandon our anxiety regarding how our behavior and choices will look to our friends, coworkers, and loved ones. Doing so won't suddenly turn us into sociopaths. Instead, it will give us the freedom to fully explore our negative thoughts and emotions, show ourself compassion, and take the necessary steps to heal and move forward.

∿

EXERCISE #11

∿

As with previous exercises, you'll need a pen and pad of paper. First, create the heading *"My Values."* Underneath it, write down every personal trait you consider important to how you work, live, and associate with others. Make it as comprehensive as possible.

Second, create the heading *"My Triggers."* Underneath it, write down everything other people do that prompts you to change your behavior. Maybe it's criticism. Perhaps it's gossip, about you or someone else. Maybe it's someone yelling at you. Or perhaps it's as simple as a frown from someone who is disappointed in you. Include everything that comes to mind.

Third, create the heading *"Recent Incidents That Triggered My Insecurity."* Try to recall every occasion in the recent past that harmed your self-image, even if only slightly.

Now, consider the incidents you've written on your

third list. Look at your first list and ask yourself *"did I feel insecure because I violated my values?"*

If the answer is yes, take steps to avoid repeating whatever you did wrong. If the answer is no (and it usually will be), acknowledge that the trigger that hurt your self-image served no useful purpose.

Doing this exercise gradually desensitizes us to others' opinions regarding our behaviors and choices. As long as we hold fast to our values, we can confidently stop fretting about what others think of us.

Time required: 20 minutes

STRATEGY #12: STOP TRYING TO MAKE EVERYONE ELSE HAPPY

" When you say yes to others, make sure you aren't saying no to yourself.

— PAULO COEHLO

Most of us feel a deep sense of satisfaction when we've made someone happy. When they smile because we've said something that improves their mood, we feel pleased. When they express delight because we done something nice for them, we feel happy ourself. In fact, research suggests that making others happy is the best way to make ourself feel the same way.[1]

Problems arise when this tendency begins to supersede our other priorities. We start to place others' happiness above our own needs.

For example, we need time to decompress after a stressful week, but agree to spend the weekend finishing a project at the office. This makes our boss happy, but creates more stress for us. Or a friend blames us for something of which we're innocent, but we apologize and express regret to appease him or her. This makes our friend happy to our own emotional detriment.

Constantly trying to make everyone else happy only leads to misery. We lose ourself in *their* priorities. We spend so much energy catering to others' needs and wants that we have none left to address our own.

In order to let go of our resentment, bitterness, frustrations, anger, judgments, regrets, and grudges, we need time and energy to reflect on them. We need to explore what we're feeling and why we're feeling it. Then, we need to do the hard work of undoing years of emotional conditioning that have caused us to cling to these things.

We cannot do this if we're continually trying to make other people happy. This proclivity not only robs us of the time and energy we need for self-reflection, but also digs us into a deeper emotional hole. We sacrifice our self-esteem and self-image on the altar of others' happiness.

The following exercise will help us to counter our inclination to make everyone else happy. By doing so, we'll give ourself the freedom and autonomy to address our own emotional needs.

EXERCISE #12

GRAB your pen and pad of paper. Create the heading *"My Priorities."* List every task and responsibility that you consider important.

For your job, think about to-do items you need to complete each day or week. Consider projects that you're expected to finish or presentations that you're expected to deliver by set deadlines. At home, reflect on the chores that need to be completed, the promises you've made to family members, and the personal projects you consider to be high priorities.

Next, create the heading *"Things I've Recently Done to Make Others Happy."* Include major things that forced you to sacrifice significant time and energy, such as helping a friend move or working over the weekend at your boss's request. Also include trivial things that required minimal time and energy, such as smiling at a friend or buying lunch for a coworker who left his or her wallet at home. Ideally, your list will be exhaustive.

Now, examine the two lists you've created. Ask yourself *"did anything on my second list prevent me from addressing anything on my first list?"* Smiling at a friend wouldn't have such an effect. But helping a friend move when a work-related deadline looms over your head may indeed do so.

The purpose of this exercise is to help us recognize when our efforts to make others happy work to our detriment. Once we're able to recognize this, we'll be better prepared (and hopefully more willing) to set healthy boundaries. These boundaries, in turn, will give us the time and energy we need to confront, resolve, and eventually release our pernicious thoughts and hurtful memories.

Time required: 15 minutes

1. Titova, Milla and Kennon, Sheldon. (2021). "Happiness comes from trying to make others feel good, rather than oneself." *The Journal of Positive Psychology.* DOI:10.1080/17439760.2021.1897867

STRATEGY #13: STOP TRYING TO MAKE YOURSELF HAPPY

 Happiness is like being cool: the harder you try the less it's going to happen. So stop trying. Start living.

— MARK MANSON

Our ongoing, sometimes relentless, pursuit of happiness does us more harm than good. This might seem counterintuitive. But hear me out. Remember when we were kids. We tried to act "hip" in front of others. We wanted to impress our friends and classmates and convince them we were cool enough to hang out with (and maybe even *too* cool). But a funny thing happened. The more we tried to seem "hip," the more unnatural we felt about our behavior. The more we tried to be cool, the less cool we felt.

Happiness works in a similar manner. The more we try to make ourself happy, the less happy we feel. Sometimes, we try so hard and behave so desperately to that end that we make ourself miserable.

To be clear, there's nothing wrong with desiring to be happy. All of us want to experience happiness. But the manner in which we try to make it happen often has the opposite effect.

One of the reasons is that our obsession with being happy causes us to overemphasize the impact of our failures. When we fail, we sometimes experience intensely negative emotions that are unwarranted by the circumstances. A study was published awhile back in the journal *Emotion* that described this tendency.[1] The researchers found that people who obsess over being happy often experience more stress as their obsession causes them to dwell on negative thoughts and emotions attached to their failures.

Another reason involves misconceived expectations. We mistakenly expect certain things to make us happy. When these things fail to do so, we feel discouraged and dejected. We might even fall into depression as we convince ourself that our happiness is unattainable.

For example, think of the person who strives to be wealthy because he or she believes that's the path to happiness. After spending a lifetime accumulating wealth, this individual discovers his or her expectation was misplaced. The discovery can feel acutely disheartening.

The truth is, happiness isn't something we can make happen — at least not in a significant way over the long run. Instead, it's something that arises from our behaviors, decisions, relationships, experiences, and circumstances. So we should focus our time and effort on these things rather than trying so hard to make ourself happy.

When we're not obsessed with our happiness, we have more liberty to acknowledge, manage, and release our negative emotions rather than avoiding them.

With that said, it's time for our next exercise.

EXERCISE #13

First, write down everything you believe would make you happy. Your list might include being attractive, wealthy, or famous (or even infamous). It may involve having a ton of free time, driving an expensive car, living in a gigantic house, or receiving positive attention from peers at your workplace. As in previous exercises, make this list as comprehensive as possible.

Second, think about the times you've felt truly happy. Try to remember the circumstances that gave rise to this feeling. Did it stem from a look of joy on your children's faces as you spent time playing with them? Did it happen while you were relaxing during a much-needed vacation? Did your happiness follow a family get-together? Briefly describe these circumstances on your pad of paper.

Now, notice how your first list contains things you have yet to achieve while your second list contains *experiences* you've already enjoyed. For example, you may expect wealth to make you happy, but it's really your children's joy during play that does so. You might think that driving a Lamborghini Huracan will make you happy, but it's actually enjoying dinner and games with family and friends that does so.

Doing this exercise reframes how we think of happiness. It erodes our assumption that we can *make* ourself happy and reinforces the idea that happiness is an aftereffect of our circumstances and experiences. Once we accept this new, healthier perspective, we can focus our attention on addressing — and ultimately letting go of — our distress, bitterness, and other exhausting and crippling emotions.

Time required: 20 minutes

---

1. McGuirk, L., Kuppens, P., Kingston, R., & Bastian, B. (2018). Does a culture of happiness increase rumination over failure? *Emotion*, 18(5), 755–764. https://doi.org/10.1037/emo0000322

STRATEGY #14: SCRUTINIZE HOW YOU MAKE DECISIONS

 Life is a matter of choices, and every choice you make makes you.

— JOHN C. MAXWELL

Many of our regrets, resentments, and grievances can be traced back to our decisions. We've made choices that we've later lamented. It's a part of life.

For example, perhaps we chose to dive headfirst into a relationship we suspected would be unhealthy for us. Over time, maybe due to toxicity, codependency, or some other unfortunate circumstance, our suspicions were confirmed. Predictably, the relationship ended in disaster, causing us to feel angry, resentful, and hurt.

Or maybe we decided to start a business despite possessing no market research showing a demand for the product or service we planned to offer. After months (or worse, years) of trying to make the business a success, we're eventually forced to close it down in failure. Naturally, we feel demoralized, pessimistic, ineffectual, and even ashamed.

In both of these hypothetical situations, note how our decisions set the stage. We *chose* to dive into an unhealthy relationship. We *chose* to start a business without evidence of demand.

On the one hand, this is encouraging news. It means we have agency. We're capable of making plans and decisions that affect our life. We're in control.

On the other hand, it underscores that the way we make decisions has an enormous impact on the outcomes we experience. If we're reckless in our choices, diving in without considering the attendant risks, we're sure to experience undesirable outcomes and the emotional pain attached to them.

In short, we often create the situations that later cause us misery. To that end, we're often responsible for the negative emotions we later struggle to let go.

Again, this is good news. We can evaluate our decision-making process and determine if we're making choices impulsively or methodically. If the latter is the case, we can make adjustments and refrain from causing ourself avoidable emotional distress and suffering along the way. If the former is the case, the changes we need to make are more foundational.

Let's don our investigator hats. In the exercise below, we'll examine how we make decisions and determine where to make practical, constructive adjustments.

EXERCISE #14

IN THIS EXERCISE, we'll make a series of statements regarding our decision-making process and assign each a rating based upon its accuracy. A rating of "1" means the statement is completely untrue while a rating of "5" means it's on the mark. At the end, we'll tally our score.

On your pad of paper, write down a value between "1" and "5" for each of the following statements:

1. I follow a carefully constructed process whenever I make a decision.
2. I determine what I want to achieve before I make a decision.
3. I take into account every factor that might affect the outcome before I make a decision.
4. I'm never surprised by the effects of my decisions.

5. When I feel uncertain about a decision, I review my process to look for errors.
6. I rely on my experience and knowledge rather than gut instinct whenever I make decisions.
7. I rarely rush my decisions.

If you scored between 30 and 35, there's not much room for improvement. You have an effective decision-making process. You're thinking carefully about your options, considering the potential risks and rewards associated with each, and choosing accordingly.

If you scored between 20 and 29, we can make positive, useful adjustments. For example, if you seldom think about what you'd like to achieve with a decision, this oversight deserves attention. If you often rush decisions, this too is an area that warrants attention.

If you scored between 10 and 19, there's plenty of room for improvement. This might involve exploring why you're often surprised by the results of your decisions. It may include thinking about ways to incorporate your experience and knowledge into your decision-making rather than relying on your gut instinct.

By improving our decision-making process, we can circumvent some of the heartache, regret, and emotional pain that might otherwise burden us. And when we're confronted by these things, we can ask ourself whether we contributed to them. Doing so acknowledges that we may have made poor choices, paving the way for us to forgive ourself and let them go.

Time required: 15 minutes

STRATEGY #15: DIAGNOSE WHY YOU'RE FEELING LAZY

 Time is free, but it's priceless. You can't own it, but you can use it. You can't keep it, but you can spend it. Once you've lost it you can never get it back.

— HARVEY MACKAY

All of us struggle with laziness. Even the most productive person you know is sometimes lazy. And this isn't always a bad thing.

The truth is, laziness can occasionally be beneficial. It gives us a chance to relax, unwind, and recharge. It can help us to manage our attentional resources and focus on things that are important to us. And sometimes, when we're being lazy, we come up with smart ways to resolve persistent issues (even if just to answer the question *"how can I fix this with minimal effort?"*).

Laziness isn't without positive effects.

The problem is, we tend to get carried away with it. We allow our laziness to continue long after we've recharged our batteries. We allow it to persist even though we're no longer coming up with creative solutions to existing problems.

This can happen for a myriad of reasons. For some, it's a simple lack of self-discipline. For others, it's disinterest in — or ambivalence toward — whatever requires their attention. Still others fear failure, feel depressed, or believe their efforts won't matter in the long run.

When our laziness persists beyond its usefulness, it begins to take a toll on our self-esteem. This starts with excuses. For example, we tell ourself that we're being lazy because we don't feel well or because the "time isn't right."

But soon, our inner critic takes over. It tries to convince us that our laziness stems from shortcomings in our character or deficits in our knowledge or ability. Before long, we begin to question our self-worth. We start to lose faith in ourself, believing that we're inadequate to the task at hand.

This downward progression in our thoughts can open the door to feelings of hopelessness, discouragement, and worse. It can eventually make us feel useless and undeserving of compassion and forgiveness — from others *and* ourself.

This hurtful self-assessment is antithetical to letting go of our negative emotions and painful memories. In fact, it *reinforces* them as we start to believe that we're unworthy of enjoying emotional freedom.

For these reasons, it's important that we figure out why we're feeling lazy when we're feeling so. It's one thing if we want to simply relax and regain our energy. It's quite another if our laziness stems from self-condemnation and unhealthy thought patterns that provoke and embolden our inner critic.

EXERCISE #15

THINK about recent incidences where you knew something needed your attention, but you decided to do nothing. Perhaps you needed to go grocery shopping, and simply chose not to do so. Maybe your vehicle needed an oil change, but you decided to stay home and watch your favorite sitcom. Or maybe you had committed to meeting friends for breakfast, but chose instead to stay in bed.

Write down your reasons.

This will require a fair bit of introspection. Most importantly, it'll require your candor and honesty. Be frank with yourself. That's the only way to gain insight into your motivations.

Following are common reasons people feel lazy (use this

list as a springboard for creating one that's unique to your experience):

- inability to ignore distractions
- unwillingness to be responsible for items/problems that need attention
- indecisiveness
- lack of interest
- feelings of inadequacy
- fear of failing to meet others' expectations
- fear of successfully meeting others' expectations
- feelings of discouragement
- feelings of sadness and depression
- feelings of pessimism and futility
- feelings of bitterness and resentment for having to be responsible for items/problems that need attention

Notice that some of these reasons suggest nothing more than a lack of discipline. But other reasons imply something deeper and more sinister. They suggest unhealthy emotions that are not only causing our inertia, but also eroding our self-esteem, self-confidence, and sense of agency.

These latter reasons deserve scrutiny. Why are we feeling this way? What is the root source of these feelings? And how do we stop feeling them?

In *Strategy #2: Identify Your Emotional State*, we discussed how our emotions — both positive and negative — prejudice our perspective and influence how we solve problems. Here, we're approaching the same issue through the lens of our lethargy and malaise.

This simple exercise can yield incredibly useful insight. It can reveal negative thought patterns that might otherwise remain hidden from us. Once they're revealed, we can calmly and bravely confront them, acknowledging them and ultimately showing ourself compassion by letting them go.

Time required: 20 minutes

STRATEGY #16: PRACTICE GRATITUDE

> He is a wise man who does not grieve for the things which he has not, but rejoices for those which he has.
>
> — EPICTETUS

We often fail to notice the good things that happen to us each day. We overlook the small moments of serendipity that benefit us. We disregard the nice things that friends, coworkers, and loved ones do for us. We take for granted the wonderful food we enjoy each day, the resources at our disposal, and the fact that we have a roof over our head.

There's a simple reason. Recall the chapter *Our Brains Are Hardwired To Survive* from *Part I*. We discussed how the mind prioritizes survival above all other concerns. This intent compels us to focus on things that might jeopardize our well-being. In short, we're always on the lookout for potential threats.

As previously noted, this is called the negativity bias. It's the way our minds are built.

As mentioned earlier, survival clearly isn't a concern for us today in the way it was for our ancestors. We rarely encounter the same types of threats and hazards. Yet, this negativity bias is difficult to abandon because it is hard-coded into us.

The problem is, when we focus on things that can go wrong rather than celebrate the good things in our life, we operate from a place of fear. This fear reinforces the emotionally painful experiences we've endured in the past. It highlights our unmet needs. It emphasizes past betrayals. It underscores our dashed expectations, painful memories, and personal grudges.

It's a constant reminder that so many things have hurt us in the past and can potentially hurt us again in the future. So we cling to the painful memories and the cynicism, distrust, and negativity attached to them. It's a survival mechanism.

Of course, this makes letting go of the past and enjoying the present almost impossible.

Fortunately, we can short circuit our negativity bias by practicing gratitude. By being mindful of everything positive that happens to us, we erode our natural fear of anything that might cause us sorrow, distress, and heartache. In doing so, we gradually rewire our brains so that it becomes easier for us to let go of the things that cause us anguish.

Practicing gratitude is simple. But it's difficult to know how and where to start if we've never done it. The exercise below will get us started on the right foot.

~

EXERCISE #16

~

I ENCOURAGE you to keep a gratitude journal. As we build this practice, you can return to it each day to reflect on what you've written and gain inspiration for future entries.

First, write down 10 things for which you're grateful. Include things both big and small. Once you begin to write, you'll likely come up with dozens of things about which you feel appreciative. But focus on 10 for now.

Second, reflect on each of the 10 items you've listed. One by one, think about how your life would be without it. For example, suppose you're thankful that you have a secure job that you genuinely enjoy. Imagine what it would feel like to have a job you loathe with an uncertain future.

Third, for each item on your list, ask yourself *"did anyone contribute to my enjoying this?"* For example, did a friend recommend you for the job you currently enjoy? Did a family member help you with a down payment for your home? Did an acquaintance teach you to play the guitar, a hobby you now relish? Write down the name of any such individual next to the item on your list.

The last step may feel uncomfortable. But I strongly encourage you to do it as it has a lot of positive effects. Express your thanks to the individuals whose names you wrote on your list. There's no need to lavish them with syrupy appreciation. Simply say "thanks." For example, you might tell your friend, *"I love the job you recommended me for. Thanks for doing that."*

This exercise encourages us to acknowledge that good things regularly happen to us, and it helps us to recognize them. In the process, we whittle away our fear of things that have the potential to cause us emotional suffering. We also become less inclined to fixate on our painful memories and more willing to let them go and enjoy the present.

Time required: 10 minutes

STRATEGY #17: ASSUME RESPONSIBILITY FOR LINGERING PROBLEMS

> There are two primary choices in life: To accept conditions as they exist, or accept the responsibility for changing them.

— DENIS WAITLEY

As important as it is to practice gratitude as a means of letting go of our emotional pain, it's also important to acknowledge existing problems. We can't ignore them. They might involve your job or workplace (e.g. tension with coworkers, missed deadlines, etc.). They may involve your personal and home life (e.g. a heated argument with your spouse, a leak in your roof, etc.).

It's natural to want to blame others for the bad things

that affect us. For example, if we miss a job-related deadline, it's not because we mismanaged our time. It's because a coworker's interruptions didn't allow us to work. If we get into an argument with our spouse, it's our spouse's fault, not our own.

This tendency to deflect blame arises for a few reasons. First, we blame others because it allows us to close the causal loop. It explains why the unfortunate circumstance happened.

Second, it allows us to create a narrative that shields us from culpability. By placing the blame on someone else, we can sidestep feeling guilty.

Third, we do it because it's easy. If we can blame someone else for whatever issue we're struggling with, we can avoid spending the time and effort necessary to examine our own contribution to it.

But there's a dark side to this habit. The more we blame others, the more we see ourself as a victim. The more we see ourself as a victim, the less agency we feel we possess. Without this sense of agency, we feel powerless to control our fate, which only increases our fixation on our frustrations, disappointments, grievances, and painful memories.

The most effective way to counter this tendency is to take responsibility for problems that affect us. This doesn't mean we immediately accept blame for such problems. Rather, we simply stop blaming *others*, recognizing that doing so is pointless. Rather than attributing our problems to those around us, we commit to taking action to resolve them.

For example, suppose we miss a job-related deadline. A coworker may have indeed repeatedly interrupted us, preventing us from working. But rather than assigning blame, it's more productive to take purposeful action toward resolving the issue — in this case, completing the task in as timely a manner as possible.

This approach requires that we change our frame of mind. For most of us, this change won't come naturally or easily. We'll almost certainly need to confront and override years of conditioning to gradually adopt this new habit. The exercise below, while simple, will prove instrumental toward that end.

~

EXERCISE #17

~

FIRST, write down every recent or current circumstance that is causing you to experience negative emotions. For example, someone at your workplace may have "accidentally" taken your lunch, making you feel angry. You may have received a speeding ticket, causing you to feel upset and disappointed. Or perhaps a friend canceled dinner plans, making you feel lonely.

Second, write down the name of the individual you instinctively want to blame for the issue. For example, write down your coworker's name for having taken your lunch. Write down the name of the police officer (or simply write "officer") for having given you a speeding ticket. Write down the name of your friend who canceled dinner plans.

Third, for each item on your list, ask yourself, *"Does blaming this person resolve this issue?"* The answer will almost certainly be "no."

Lastly, write down a single action you can take to either resolve the issue or lessen the likelihood of it recurring. For example, you might be able to store your lunch in a different location. You can decide to drive the speed limit in the future. You could always have a "Plan B" when making plans with this particular friend (e.g. *"If Tony cancels on me, I'll read that novel I've been looking forward to reading."*)

Regularly doing this exercise trains our minds to take responsibility for problems that inconvenience us. In doing so, it also encourages us to assume responsibility for our emotional pain. We're not blaming ourself for it. Importantly, we're not blaming *anyone*. Instead, we're granting that we have the capacity to acknowledge our pain, deal with it rather than avoid it, and ultimately let it go.

Time required: 20 minutes

STRATEGY #18: EMBRACE YOUR LACK OF CONTROL

 You have power over your mind — not outside events. Realize this, and you will find strength.

— MARCUS AURELIUS

It's a natural instinct to want to control everything that affects us. We want to feel as if we're at the helm of our ship, managing our life by exerting influence over our circumstances and the people around us. But this sense of control over external factors is largely a delusion. And it's one that inflicts an emotional cost.

For example, recall the last time you were stuck in traffic. You had no influence over the situation and so were forced to wait for the traffic to clear. While waiting, powerless to change your circumstances, you may have felt frustrated and anxious.

Or recall a past relationship where your partner was unfaithful. You had no control over his or her actions. You could only trust they would remain committed to the relationship. When that trust was broken, you were left to deal with the emotional aftermath.

Although craving control is a natural instinct, it fundamentally impairs our ability to let go of our anger, disappointments, resentments, and regrets. It causes us to fixate on our negative experiences, unable to reconcile why they occurred. After all, if we're truly in control of our circumstances, we must be at fault when things go poorly. But the idea of self-sabotage is anathema to our nature.

We want life to be predictable. But the reality is, life is often random. Bad things occasionally happen to us regardless of our decisions and actions. If we hope to experience freedom from our negative thoughts and emotional burdens, we must come to terms with our inherent *lack* of control.

We can control our choices. We can control our thoughts. We can control how we treat others. And we can control how we respond to events, people, and other external stimuli. But we have *limited* control over our environment, other people's actions, and events that adversely affect us.

If we can relinquish our desire for control, embracing the fact that it's ultimately an illusion, life's randomness becomes easier to tolerate. We'll become more willing and able to recognize that many of our negative experiences stem from factors beyond our influence. Accordingly, much of the emotional pain we feel as a result of these experiences will become easier to manage and ultimately release.

~

EXERCISE #18

~

FIRST, create the heading *"Things I Cannot Control."* Underneath it, write down a list of things over which you have minimal influence. Focus on people and your environment. Note that your list may become lengthy. The lengthier, the better.

Following are a few ideas to get you started with regard to people...

- how people feel about me
- how people behave around me
- how people treat me
- the decisions people make
- the thoughts people entertain

And here are a few ideas with regard to your environment...

- the weather
- the economy
- traffic
- getting older
- the past
- natural phenomena (earthquakes, pandemics, etc.)

Neither list is exhaustive, of course. Again, they're designed to get you started.

Second, create the heading *"Things I DO Control."* Underneath it, write down everything over which you *can* exert influence. As with our first list, this one may also become lengthy. As you'll see in the third step, the more things you write down, the better.

Here are some ideas to get your creative juices flowing...

- how I spend my time
- where I devote my focus and energy
- my behavior
- how I treat those around me
- whether I hold grudges
- the principles and values I uphold
- the level of compassion I show to others
- the level of compassion I show to myself
- the decision to be a better spouse, friend, sibling, employee, etc.
- how I react to what others say and do

Third, review each item on your first list. As you do so, ask yourself *"do I feel attached to any outcome that stems from this item?"* If the answer is "yes," investigate the reasons. For example, does your attachment arise from ego and pride? Does it flow from faulty expectations? Does it come about because you haven't allowed for the randomness of life?

Now, review each item on your second list. Notice that all of them involve your attitude, behavior, priorities, goals, and convictions. These are the things you control.

The fourth and final step of this exercise is to develop a mindset of non-attachment to outcomes associated with items on your first list. Fair warning: this will take time. Changing our frame of mind is always a struggle because we must unravel years of programming.

Be patient with — and compassionate toward — yourself. Celebrate small victories. For example, the next time you're stuck in traffic, try to detach your emotions from the situation. If you're successful, praise yourself.

This exercise, along with adopting a mindset that focuses on things we can control, aids us in letting go of our emotional burdens. Once we recognize that much of the psychological pain we carry stems from things outside our influence, we can more confidently surrender them and move forward.

Time required to complete steps 1 through 3: 15 minutes

Time required to complete step 4: Several weeks, and perhaps even months

STRATEGY #19: STOP KEEPING SCORE IN RELATIONSHIPS

 The greatest obstacle to connecting with our joy is resentment.

— PEMA CHODRON

Our relationships are the source of much of our happiness. The camaraderie we share with our coworkers, the companionship and support we enjoy with our friends, and the love we feel for our families bring us a deep sense of satisfaction.

But our relationships can also be the source of much of our emotional anguish. Duplicity, crushed expectations, and unaddressed grievances can leave us feeling betrayed, let down, and angry.

If we can let go of the frustration, bitterness, and

resentment we feel toward others, we can more effectively confront the issues that prompted these feelings. Unfortunately, we tend to hold on to these things. This often happens because we keep a "relationship scorecard." This scorecard keeps track of the positive and negative things our coworkers, friends, and loved ones do.

Everything is placed on this scorecard. This includes minor "infractions," such as rude comments, irritating texts, and displeasing opinions. Every trivial transgression that irks us makes it onto this scorecard. And unsurprisingly, due to our negativity bias, we overlook many of the positive things people do. So our scorecard ends up being unfairly lopsided. It thus provides an inaccurate portrayal of who's "ahead" or "behind."

But the *real* problem is that keeping a scorecard always leads to bitterness and resentment. The relationship, whether it's with a coworker, friend, or family member, becomes a competition.

And there is never a winner.

The other person inevitably feels taken for granted and unappreciated. And we ultimately convince ourself that we're doing the heavy lifting, putting in more than our fair share of time, effort, and emotional capital.

The negative emotions that spring from this dynamic not only cause the relationship to deteriorate, but are also difficult for us to release. We dwell on them. We cling to them. And as they fester, they cause us to feel more and more resentment and regret.

Today, let's commit to abandoning these scorecards.

Let's pledge to stop keeping track of whether the people in our life are "pulling their weight." The exercise below will help us to start enjoying scoreless relationships, and thereby let go of pointless grudges, aggravations, and hurt feelings.

EXERCISE #19

WRITE down the name of someone with whom you spend significant time. This can be your spouse, a close friend, or a coworker.

Next, create a list of things this individual has recently done or said that displeased you. For example, did your spouse neglect to wash the dishes? Did a friend share an opinion that you found vexing? Was a coworker late to a meeting you scheduled for the two of you? Write it down, regardless of how trivial it now seems.

Now, create a list of traits you appreciate in this person. Here's a short list to get you started:

- positive attitude
- great sense of humor
- willing to listen
- slow to judge
- quick to forgive
- eager to take responsibility

- loyal
- truthful
- consistent
- enthusiastic

Make your list as comprehensive as possible.

Lastly, review the list of things this individual did that displeased you. Keeping in mind his or her positive traits, ask yourself *"how serious is this issue to me in the long run?"* Provide your answer by assigning each item on your first list a number between 1 and 10.

Quantifying our displeasure after privately acknowledging our appreciation for this person has a clarifying effect. It shows us that while our irritation may be valid, it's imprudent to hold on to it given all that we enjoy and admire about this person.

Time required: 15 minutes

STRATEGY # 20: STOP MAKING UNNECESSARY COMMITMENTS

> I've screwed up and I've overcommitted and it's typical of me.

— ROBERT METCALFE

It's easy to overcommit these days. There are more demands than ever on our time, attention, and other resources. Many of us find ourself so busy trying to meet our obligations that we are left with little time to address our own needs or pursue our own interests.

It's exhausting. In fact, it's a recipe for feeling stressed and burned out.

But there's *another* issue with overcommitting, and it's a particularly problematic one because it's so easy to overlook. When we devote our attentional resources to a seemingly endless list of "duties," we rob ourself of the energy we need to explore our emotional burdens.

And if we don't fully explore them, we cannot truly resolve them and let them go.

To be sure, each of us has commitments that we cannot avoid. Some are related to our job. Others involve our family. And some are associated with other aspects of our life, such as volunteering to help nonprofit organizations, contributing time and energy to our churches, and maintaining side work. We cannot abandon these commitments in good conscious.

But we *can* avoid committing ourself to tasks and roles that we consider to be lower in priority. We can start saying "no" more often. We can begin to edit our life so that we honor our high-priority duties while leaving ourself sufficient time to manage our emotional health.

It's difficult to say no when we're accustomed to saying yes. But the upside is that we'll avoid overextending ourself. Instead of spending all of our time and energy helping others get what *they* want out of life, we can reserve these resources for our own priorities.

How do we stop filling our calendars and to-do lists with unnecessary commitments? The exercise that follows provides a simple plan.

EXERCISE #20

LET'S CREATE A TIME BUDGET. We only have 24 hours each day. It's helpful to recognize how some of this time is already committed.

First, create the heading *"Personal and Home Care."* Underneath it, write the following items:

- sleep
- bathing/grooming
- exercise
- meals & meal prep
- chores
- family time

Second, write down the amount of time you spend on each item each day. Focus on the ideal. For example, you might sleep four hours per day, but the ideal is seven (this varies by age). You might spend no time exercising each day, but recognize you should do so. Here's what your list might look like following this step:

- sleep — 7 hours
- bathing/grooming — 45 minutes
- exercise — 20 minutes
- meals & meal prep — 2 hours
- chores — 30 minutes
- family time — 90 minutes

This totals a bit over 12 hours. This means you have 12 hours left in your budget. Now, create the heading *"Work"* and go through the same process. Here's what your list might look like:

- commute — 1 hour
- time at job — 8 hours

This totals 9 hours. We have 3 hours left. Next, create the heading *"Other Areas."* This will encompass things like volunteer work, time spent at church, and helping clients via a side business. If you spend time on such things only once or twice a week, simply divide the time you spend by seven to calculate a daily average. Here's a hypothetical list:

- volunteer work — 3 hours per week or approximately 30 minutes per day
- church — 3 hours per week or approximately 30 minutes per day
- side business — 1 hour per day

This totals 2 hours. We have 1 hour left.

Now, write down your hobbies and interests. For example, do you play the guitar? Do you regularly spend time in prayer or meditation? Do you enjoy reading self-improvement books? Do you relish watching Netflix?

Remember, we only have 1 hour left in our budget. How will we spend it?

This exercise serves two purposes. First, it reveals how

much of our time is already committed, even if we don't realize it. Second, it underscores the fact that overcommitting means siphoning away time from important areas of our life.

When we acknowledge that our time and energy is limited, and can see these limitations in plain view on paper, it becomes easier to say no. And the more often we say no, the more time we have for self-analysis. We give ourself more freedom to examine, resolve, and ultimately release the emotional pain that weighs us down.

Time required: 10 minutes

STRATEGY #21: LEARN TO FORGIVE YOURSELF AND OTHERS

66 Take stock of everyone who has ever wronged you in any way, regardless of how severe or recent it may have been, and make the choice to let go. Forgiveness is an act of the heart.

— WAYNE DYER

Much of the emotional pain we bear stems from unfair treatment at the hands of others. We feel hurt, betrayed, forgotten, or disrespected. These feelings turn into resentment, which we hold on to as a way to protect ourself. If we resent the person responsible for our anguish, we're less inclined to be emotionally vulnerable around them.

A lot of the emotional suffering we experience also

stems from how we treat ourself. We are our harshest critic. When we err, make poor choices, or fail to perform up to our standards, we castigate ourself. We beat ourself up for our failings and shortcomings. This leads to guilt and shame, emotions that needlessly wound our self-image, acting like shackles that constrict our freedom.

The solution is to adopt an attitude of forgiveness. We must be willing to forgive others as well as ourself.

This is easier said than done, of course. Forgiving others makes us vulnerable to them. We dread being hurt by them again, so we're disinclined to pardon them.

Forgiving ourself is no easier. We're reluctant to let ourself off the hook because, deep down, we believe we should be perfect. We set unreasonably high standards for ourself. We give ourself no latitude to make mistakes. We see self-forgiveness as weakness, and so we withhold it. But self-reproach doesn't make us stronger. It just pummels our ego to the point that we feel that we can't do anything right.

When we adopt an attitude of forgiveness toward others, we can more easily move on from past hurts. Yes, we make ourself more vulnerable. And no, forgiving others won't necessarily change their behavior toward us. But it allows us to let go of our bitterness and resentment. This offers its own rewards. A small, but growing body of research shows that forgiving others can reduce our stress and increase our productivity.[1] But most importantly, doing so can help to end our emotional suffering.

When we adopt an attitude of *self*-forgiveness, we can

more easily let go of the shame and guilt we feel regarding our mistakes, choices, and poor performance. We stop feeling worthless and ineffectual. Instead, our self-compassion recognizes our humanity and innate fallibility. We accept that we make mistakes. We become less likely to dwell on them and less inclined to entertain the negative emotions that arise from them.

As mentioned, forgiveness doesn't come easy for most of us. We have to work at it. The following exercise will help. It gives us an opportunity to reflect on our emotions whenever we feel hurt by others or disappointed in ourself. It encourages us to question whether these emotions are doing us more harm than good. The insight we gain will gradually help to free us of the heartache, resentment, shame, and other toxic feelings that are holding us back.

∾

EXERCISE #21

∾

THIS IS A TWO-PART EXERCISE. The first part will focus on adopting a forgiving attitude toward others. The second part will focus on adopting a similar attitude toward ourself.

First, write down the name of someone whose behavior recently angered or hurt you. Next, write down exactly what this individual did or said that evoked this response.

Now, describe the emotions you experienced. Sadness? Outrage? Shame? Whatever the case, write them down.

Second, create a list that describes how these emotions influence your behavior. Here's an example list:

- I'm unable to focus on my work
- I'm apprehensive around this person
- I'm less likely to share my opinions
- I feel discouraged regarding my goals
- I'm unable to be present with loved ones

Third, create a list that describes how you'll feel if you forgive this person and move on. Here's an example list:

- I'll feel more at peace
- I'll feel less anxious
- I'll feel less hostile
- I'll feel more empathetic
- I'll feel more compassionate

Lastly, review these two lists side by side. Weigh the benefits of forgiving the person against the drawbacks of bearing a grudge and holding on to resentment.

Writing down our emotions, along with how they influence our frame of mind and behavior, makes it easier to examine their impact. It helps us to be more objective. Consequently, we're able to more quickly recognize that the upside to forgiving others and moving on far eclipses any upside to holding on to resentment, anger, and shame.

Now, let's shift our focus to *self*-forgiveness. We'll take a similar approach. First, describe a recent incident that prompted you to criticize yourself. Next, write down the emotions you experienced. Guilt? Despair? Embarrassment? As before, whatever the case, write them down.

Second, create a list that describes how these emotions influence your behavior. Here's an example list:

- I'm less likely to take risks
- I'm more likely to doubt my abilities
- I'm more likely to give up
- I'm more likely to withdraw from others and isolate myself
- I'm less likely to express my needs to others

Third, create a list that describes how you'll feel if you forgive yourself. Here's an example list:

- I'll feel more confident
- I'll experience a greater sense of freedom
- I'll be able to take action without fear
- I'll waste less time and energy on incidents I can't change
- I'll enjoy healthier, more compassionate relationships

Lastly, weigh the benefits of forgiving yourself against the downsides of continued self-condemnation. We can quickly see that forgiving ourself is the smoothest path toward releasing our despair, guilt, and other emotional burdens.

Time required: 30 minutes

---

1. Toussaint, Loren and Worthington, Everett L. (2018). "Forgiveness Working: Forgiveness, Health, and Productivity in the Workplace." American Journal of Health Promotion. DOI: 10.1177/0890117116662312

BONUS STRATEGY #1: DEVELOP "EMOTIONAL DIVERSITY"

     Negative emotions like loneliness, envy, and guilt have an important role to play in a happy life; they're big, flashing signs that something needs to change.

— GRETCHEN RUBIN

You've no doubt met people who seemed perpetually and exclusively happy. They always smile, always laugh, and always seem in good cheer. They're unflaggingly upbeat. And they can be a lot to handle if they catch us before we drink our first cup of coffee in the morning.

The idea that they might be holding on to some type of

emotional pain seems unfathomable given their constant high spirits.

But it turns out they may not be as happy as they appear. Psychologists are discovering that experiencing a *variety* of emotions, both good *and bad,* is better for our long-term emotional health.[1] They call it "emotional diversity" (or emodiversity).

Emotional diversity works in a manner similar to the stock market. Diversifying our investment funds into a variety of stocks helps us to weather downturns in any one particular stock. It protects our investment portfolio from catastrophe. (This is the reason many people invest in mutual funds.) In the same way, emodiversity helps us to endure experiences that might otherwise lead to emotional devastation. It protects our *emotional* portfolio.

For example, consider an individual who is always cheerful. If he or she truly experiences only positive emotions (e.g. joy, happiness, etc.), a single, major negative event, such as getting fired or divorced could ruin her long-term emotional state. By contrast, someone who regularly experiences a wide range of emotions, from joy and happiness to sadness and frustration, is better prepared to endure such an event.

Emotional diversity helps us to let go of our distressing memories, painful regrets, and upsetting grievances. We experience an array of emotions that makes us more adaptable to our circumstances. We become more resilient to the negative thoughts and feelings that might otherwise monopolize our headspace. Rather than obsessing over our emotional pain, we become more comfortable confronting its source, managing our feelings regarding it, and finally letting those feelings go.

The following exercise will reinforce the importance of developing emodiversity and help us to gain insight into what triggers the emotions we experience.

BONUS EXERCISE #1

First, create a list of emotions you've recently experienced. Ideally, it'll include emotions that fall across a wide spectrum, from happiness to sadness, from anger to delight. The greater the range, the better.

Second, briefly describe the incident that prompted each emotion. For example, were you angered by something a coworker said to you? Were you overjoyed to get a raise at your job? Were you saddened to learn a close friend was relocating to another country?

Third, review the distribution of emotions on your list. Does it seem balanced or does it disproportionately favor negative or positive emotions? If your list favors one or the other, review the incidents that triggered them. Do any patterns stand out that suggest emotional fragility, such as how you react to disparaging comments from coworkers?

This exercise is designed to improve our self-awareness

regarding the range of emotions we experience. If we discover that we rarely experience emotions outside a limited band, we can look for opportunities to broaden our emotional diversity.

For example, if we usually feel angry and resentful, we can do things that make us feel good, such as praising others. If we're usually happy, we can take the time to acknowledge things that make us unhappy rather than simply avoiding them.

Time required: 20 minutes

---

1. Quoidbach, Jordi, et. al. (2014) "Emodiversity and the emotional ecosystem." Journal of Experimental Psychology: General. vol. 143, no. 6, pp. 2057–2066. PMID: 25285428 DOI: 10.1037/a0038025

BONUS STRATEGY #2: MANAGE YOUR EMOTIONAL INVESTMENT IN EXPECTED OUTCOMES

" It is easier to make our wishes conform to our means than to make our means conform to our wishes.

— ROBERT E. LEE

We expect a lot from ourself and others. When our expectations are unmet, we experience disappointment, frustration, and even anger. We believe a certain outcome should happen. We become invested in it. When it fails to materialize as we imagine it, our patience evaporates and our inner critic denounces everyone involved (if only in our heads).

That's a lot of pressure to place on ourself and other people. And because mistakes, poor decisions, and misdeeds are inevitable (we're human, after all), it's a recipe for resentment. This resentment can grow to the point that we become perpetually bitter. We begin to expect failure, from ourself and others, while maintaining our rigid standards.

It's a vicious cycle. As it repeats, it reinforces a negative attitude and encourages us to hold on to it despite its harmful effect on our emotional well-being. Prolonging this state increases our stress, impairs our objectivity, and can even lead to depression. Preoccupied with this negativity, we fixate on our disappointments, frustrations, and judgments, unable to let them go.

We must short circuit this cycle. We need to manage our expectations lest they manage us and wreck our mental health in the process.

It won't be easy. And it'll take time. But if you're willing to invest the time and effort, you'll find that managing your expectations will lessen the potency of the emotional turmoil you experience when things don't go as planned. In fact, it will render irrelevant many of the *sources* of that emotional pain. And ultimately, it will ease the process of releasing it.

～

BONUS EXERCISE #2

～

WRITE down a list of recent incidents that made you feel angry, frustrated, or disappointed. Describe the events, behaviors, and decisions that prompted these feelings.

For example, you may have felt disappointed when a friend arrived late to a scheduled lunch. Or perhaps your spouse neglected to take out the trash, causing you to feel frustrated. Maybe a coworker failed to complete his or her part of a project, creating more work for you (and angering you as a result).

The negative emotions you experienced were based on your expectations. But they actually stem from being emotionally invested in a particular outcome (e.g. your friend arriving on time for lunch). When that outcome didn't happen, you reacted negatively (if only privately).

The purpose of this exercise is to highlight this fact and help us to separate our expectations from our emotional investment in how things ultimately occur. In doing so, we can improve our ability to adapt when our expectations are unmet. We may experience anger, frustration, and disappointment, but we're less likely to be consumed by them. By being less emotionally invested in a particular outcome, we're better able to let these feelings go when they surface.

Time required: 15 minutes

BONUS STRATEGY #3: QUESTION THE ACCURACY OF YOUR PERSONAL NARRATIVES

 Understand and challenge your personal narrative. Narratives become choices and actions — which become your life.

— BRYANT H. MCGILL

O ur mind invents stories to make sense of our experiences. These stories are supposed to help explain why things happen and the roles we played in making them happen. It's our brain's attempt to "close the loop." It wants to assign a causal relationship between events and triggers. So it creates personal narratives to accomplish this goal.

The problem is, these narratives are usually off target.

Our brain is less concerned about accuracy than it is about attributing causality.

These narratives reinforce our cognitive biases. If we entertain a self-serving bias — attributing positive experiences to our actions and negative experiences to externalities — our personal narratives will reflect it.

For example, suppose we take an exam and receive a good grade. Our self-serving bias might attribute the grade to our intelligence, proficient test-taking skills, or the fact that we buckled down and studied. Our brain will thus create a narrative that we're smart, good at taking tests, and naturally diligent.

If we entertain a modesty bias — attributing positive experiences to externalities and negative experiences to our actions — this too will be reflected in our brain's narratives.

For example, we may attribute our good grade to the fact that the exam was too easy. Or perhaps the professor was amazingly effective at teaching the material. Our brain will create a narrative that supports these details (e.g. we were lucky to have this professor).

When *bad* things happen to us, our brain will often create narratives that suggest we are to blame. It will imply that something about our character caused the unfortunate incident. Here, it's important to remember that the brain isn't concerned with accuracy. It just wants to close the loop.

For example, suppose we take an exam and do poorly on it. Our brain will create a narrative to explain the reason(s). This narrative might suggest that we're stupid, unable to focus, or simply bad at taking exams. If we entertain it, we risk fixating on these traits, wrongly assuming they're a part of our identity. This is the path toward self-condemnation and despair.

If we *question* this narrative, we'll notice that it's inaccurate. Our poor performance on the exam may be attributable to feeling exhausted, being stressed, or having misinterpreted the material. Questioning the narrative reveals its dishonesty. Once it is revealed as false, we're less inclined to fixate on our supposed shortcomings. Instead, we can let the unfortunate incident go and move on.

The following exercise is a simple one. But don't underestimate its usefulness.

~

BONUS EXERCISE #3

~

FIRST, describe one of your regrets. Perhaps you allowed an important friendship to crumble. Maybe you neglected to stand up for yourself when others unfairly blamed you for something. Or perhaps you regret not learning a second language. Whatever the regret, write it down.

Second, describe the narrative your brain created to explain this particular regret. For example, did it suggest that you're a bad friend? Did it insinuate· that you're cowardly? Did it propose that you're lazy?

Third, simply ask yourself *"is this narrative true?"*

You'll find that asking this question will usually reveal that your brain and inner critic are trying to peddle a false account. For example, perhaps the friendship crumbled because your friend failed to return your calls. Maybe you neglected to stand up for yourself because your attention was focused on more urgent matters. Perhaps you haven't yet learned a second language because you prefer to devote your limited time to your family.

When we train ourself to question our personal narratives, we're less likely to get trapped in a cycle of self-recrimination. We can objectively review why an unfortunate event happened to us without instinctively blaming and berating ourself for it. This allows us to let it go, along with the attendant regret, and get on with our life.

Time required: 15 minutes

FINAL THOUGHTS ON THE ART OF LETTING GO

~

It's natural for us to hold on to our past. We remember good times with fondness, reliving events that brought us true joy and happiness. We recall bad times with a wistful nostalgia, replaying incidents that caused us to feel sad, angry, or lonely.

Our memories inform our life. They allow us to travel back in time, learn from the past, and make use of that insight in the present (and future).

But it's easy to become trapped by the past. Painful memories, and the negative emotions they evoke, haunt us and hold us back. Left unresolved, they cling to us like a wet garment, causing us to obsess over things we cannot change. Regret becomes our constant companion, preventing us from enjoying true emotional freedom.

I wrote *The Art of Letting GO* to help you thwart this

oppressive, unnecessarily cruel mental process. My intent was to give you the tools you need to finally silence the relentless voice of self-reproach and condemnation and instead show yourself compassion, empathy, and patience. I'm convinced this is the way to enjoy healthier relationships, a more gratifying career, and ultimately a more productive and rewarding life.

We've come a long way since the first chapter. We've discussed a great many ideas and concepts. We've covered numerous strategies that you can use starting *today* and start releasing the emotional pain you've struggled with.

If you've been doing the exercises along the way, you're already on the path to enjoying life with less stress, less resentment, less regret, and less mental anguish. Kudos to you!

If you have yet to do the exercises, you're in for a treat. They require time, attention, and energy, but you'll find that they'll help you to finally let go of the negative thoughts and emotions that burden you.

One final note… I encourage you to revisit *The Art of Letting GO* whenever you're feeling angry, depressed, or downtrodden by life. You don't necessarily have to read the entire book again. Rather, simply look through the table of contents and revisit the section that resonates with you in that moment.

And with that, I wish you all the happiness you desire and deserve. Enjoy the journey!

DID YOU ENJOY READING THE ART OF LETTING GO?

∽

Thanks so much for taking the time to read *The Art Of Letting GO*. I greatly appreciate that you chose to spend some of your limited time with me.

If you enjoyed reading *The Art Of Letting GO*, would you do me a small favor? Would you leave a short review for the book at Amazon? A sentence or two about something you liked would mean the world to me. Your words will encourage other folks to read the book.

One last thing before we part ways. I plan to write a few more books over the next twelve months. I'll likely release each of them at a steep discount for a limited time; you'll be able to grab each one for less than $1.

If you'd like to be notified when these books are released, and take advantage of the discounted price, be sure to join my mailing list. You'll also receive my 40-page PDF ebook titled *Catapult Your Productivity! The Top 10 Habits You Must Develop to Get More Things Done.*

You can join my list at the following address:

http://artofproductivity.com/free-gift/

I'll also send you my best productivity and time management tips via my email newsletter. You'll receive tips and tactics on beating procrastination, creating morning routines, avoiding burnout, and developing razor-sharp focus, along with many other productivity hacks!

If you have questions or would like to share a tip, technique, or mind hack that has made a positive difference in your life, please feel free to reach out to me at damon@artofproductivity.com. I'd love to hear about it!

Until next time,

Damon Zahariades
http://artofproductivity.com

ABOUT THE AUTHOR

Damon Zahariades is a corporate refugee who endured years of unnecessary meetings, drive-by chats with coworkers, and a distraction-laden work environment before striking out on his own. Today, in addition to writing a growing catalog of time management and productivity books, he's the showrunner for the productivity blog ArtofProductivity.com.

In his spare time, he enjoys playing chess, poker, and the occasional video game with friends. And he continues to promise himself that he'll start playing the guitar again.

Damon lives in Southern California with his beautiful, supportive wife and their affectionate, quirky, and sometimes mischievous dog. He's looking wistfully at his 50th birthday in the rearview mirror.

OTHER BOOKS BY DAMON ZAHARIADES

How to Make Better Decisions

14 proven tactics to overcome indecision, consistently make smart choices, and create a rewarding life in the process!

The Mental Toughness Handbook

The definitive, step-by-step guide to developing mental toughness! Exercises included!

To-Do List Formula

Finally! Discover how to create to-do lists that work!

The Art Of Saying NO

Are you fed up with people taking you for granted? Learn how to set boundaries, stand your ground, and inspire others' respect in the process!

The Procrastination Cure

Discover how to take quick action, make fast decisions, and finally overcome your inner procrastinator!

Fast Focus

Here's a proven system that'll help you to ignore distractions, develop laser-sharp focus, and skyrocket your productivity!

The 30-Day Productivity Plan

Need a daily action plan to boost your productivity? This 30-day guide is the solution to your time management woes!

The 30-Day Productivity Plan - VOLUME II

30 MORE bad habits that are sabotaging your time management - and how to overcome them one day at a time!

The Time Chunking Method

It's one of the most popular time management strategies used today. Triple your productivity with this easy 10-step system.

80/20 Your Life!

Achieve more, create more, and enjoy more success. How to get more done with less effort and change your life in the process!

Small Habits Revolution

Change your habits to transform your life. Use this simple, effective strategy for adopting any new habit you desire!

Morning Makeover

Imagine waking up excited, energized, and full of self-confidence. Here's how to create morning routines that lead to explosive success!

The Joy Of Imperfection

Finally beat perfectionism, silence your inner critic, and overcome your fear of failure!

The P.R.I.M.E.R. Goal Setting Method

An elegant 6-step system for achieving extraordinary results in every area of your life!

Digital Detox

Disconnect to reconnect. Discover how to unplug and enjoy a more mindful, meaningful, and rewarding life!

For a complete list, please visit

http://artofproductivity.com/my-books/

Made in the USA
Columbia, SC
26 March 2023

14310758R00107